Robin Williams Is My Uncle:
And Other Stories We Possess

Cathy Borders

Shape & Color Books

Robin Williams Is My Uncle:
And Other Stories We Possess

Copyright © 2025 Cathy Borders
Content compiled for publication by
Shape & Color Books.
First published by Shape & Color Books 2025.
All rights reserved.

No part of this publication may be reproduced or transmitted in any form or by any means, electronic or mechanical, including photocopy, recording, or an information storage and retrieval system, without permission in writing from the publisher.
The right of Cathy Borders to be identified as the author of this work has been asserted by her in accordance with the Copyright, Designs and Patent Act 1988

ISBN: 979-8-9986267-0-8

CathyBorders.com
ShapeandColorBooks.com

For Rufus.

And for Robin Williams.

...

The symbolic stories we tell—no matter how much they help us navigate the real—are dismissed as trivial or disdained lies. But these seeming trifles can transmit higher truths, in part because they conceal as much as they reveal, challenging us to unpack the wisdom that drives their plots.

– Maria Tatar

...

Not everything inside of you is yours.

– Anne Boyer

...

There's something so wonderful about a cartoon that you can sit with your child and just laugh like crazy.

– Robin Williams

...

My uncle died the same time Robin Williams did.

Give or take.

He was my uncle by marriage, I didn't know him, not really.

I mean, I didn't know Robin Williams either but.

Confined children finish all sentences with the word "but," Dodie Bellamy writes. I copied that into my notebook. Now I'm gifting it to you.

I don't really know much about either of their deaths. They said Robin hanged himself. They said it was depression. Then they said it was dementia.

I heard my uncle crashed his truck into a tree, or drove into a lake. But maybe his heart just stopped, I heard that too. I've not gone looking for any of the details. It seems none of my business.

Anyway, facts in my family move. Like Robin's Genie, they're vaporous, they change shape midair.

Genie meaning jinn, ifrit, demon. We're not sure they're to be trusted.

Like the demons in my muscles, what's real?

What's mine?

They say when someone conjures a demon, they're actually bringing out a force from inside themself.

Please, don't worry so much. Because in the end, none of us have very long on this earth. Life is fleeting, says a Robin meme. (Impossibly, it's the ten-year anniversary of his death.)

My cat is dying. My dæmon, my familiar. My princess sidekick, my animus. Rufus was born on my bed half a lifetime ago and now he is dying.

I felt the earth quake when my mother's sister fell to the floor as the box with her husband's body passed hers. My mother ran out of the funeral parlor, *I can't take this!* she had said. The truth rushed her in a wave of awful and she fled to the safety of our car. My aunt's adult children picked her up off the floor, or attempted to, her knees buckled and she howled like an animal.

Once, I saw a neighborhood goose howl through the quiet middle of the night. They mate for life, Canada geese. Across our snowdropped suburb she walked, feathers outstretched like a vampire turning into a bat. She walked and she sang her nightmare song through the unfenced yards. All the dirty snow, pocked and mired with gray pointlessness, must have looked grotesque to her, all the straight, unnatural lines. All the foreign plants from Home Depot, all the stiff yard signs and manufactured mulch, the chemicals deep in the soil. She wailed her way down the uncanny block and I wonder how many others got out of bed to see what that was.

As Genie changes shape midair, he replicates moments in metaphor. This is him explaining himself. Because words aren't enough.

Because language and its grammars cannot contain all of human feeling.

Sometimes, we need a third thing.

As Genie, Robin is Aladdin's Merlin. He is the Magician guiding our Fool into Jasmine's bed.

He will play some version of this role over and over and over again.

This virile, avuncular figure of his takes several deranged shapes, from alien to sailor to fruit bat to nanny to robot to penguin. From dead poets to dead presidents.

He also loves the *kid trapped in an adult body* archetype.

Or the *Ope! Suddenly Dad* trope.

There is something beguiling about this teacher that doesn't want to grow up. And yet, must.

His oeuvre is like a rainbow bridge to adulthood.

This in-between person, so familiar, so alien.

I want to relate him to Uncle Traveling Matt, out there with the silly creatures, but he is the ultimate silly creature.

Whimsically, he speaks incessantly about sex, death, honor, and meaning. He gets away with it because he's fast. He gets away with it because he's brilliant. He gets away with it as jesters do.

Where be your gibes now your
gambols? your songs? your flashes of merriment,
that were wont to set the table on a roar? Not one
now, to mock your own grinning? quite chap-fallen?

He is a piece of work, Robin, both noble in reason and infinite in faculty.

In form and moving how express and admirable.

He is not unwilling to sacrifice himself for the children, for the little boy that looks up to him.

He is not unwilling to hand down the sword, or take the fall, or corrupt the youth.

Socrates drinks the hemlock, Mr. Keating loses his job.

None of the actors knew who Pan was going to pick. When Robin gave the sword to Thud, the boys' reactions were genuine.

Rufio would not have bequeathed his sword to Thud Butt.

One imagines a renaissance under Thud, an era of art and diplomacy, an end to the child snatching. May ever he reign.

Objectified, Genie's lamp is brother to the sword Arthur pulls from the stone.

Because Genie is a weapon, he is a magical force to utilize at will.

Infinite cosmic power! Itty bitty living space.

> *O God, I could be bounded in a nut shell and count myself a king of infinite space.*

Thinking of his *King of Everything*. A literal god.

Cogito ergo est, the king says. *I think therefore you is.*

Great things can happen when you use that big dick energy.

Thinking now of Billy Crystal squinking his eye into the camera and saying of Robin, *He had the biggest set of balls ever on the stage.*

Robin's humor was alive. It moved. He grabbed an image, a snapshot of a stereotype, then commented on it with an interpretation of another image, which effectively was a response to what he'd just seen, done. His jokes were like babbling streams of improvised thoughts.

Like how Sartre says, or how Beckett shows, that in consciousness one image always (endlessly unto death) begets another.

So it is with Robin's jokes.

And so it is with Genie's form. His ethereal body changes shape to suit the metaphors as he says them. A perfect mimetic harmony of image and artist.

Meaning, he uses his body to tell stories.

Funny, isn't it?

The stories trapped in our bodies.

Some of them are not even ours, and still, and yet, the body keeps the score.

My three wishes would be to heal my migraines and such; to have enough money to just write; and to not be allergic to bananas. Knowing me, though, I'd probably never make my third wish. I'd save it like the last drops of the blue Exotic Bouquet body spray in my closet.

This is assuming I couldn't ask for great health and longevity for everyone I love, including Rufus. That seems as though it's against Genie's moral code. He won't alter another's body without consent. As his objection to not making another fall in love is ethical, this seems similar. Maybe the health and longevity of someone who can consent is okay, but it would probably count as one wish per person. Much like that time he fished an unconscious Al out of the sea.

Deciphering what's inappropriate will always be a philosophical quandary. It will never not be a question of censorship and power.

Alas, Rufus is destined, as we all are, to cross the rainbow bridge.

Bridges, the restaurant from *Mrs. Doubtfire,* has a letter framed on its walls: *Your Bridges was a joy to cross. May it last forever. All my love.*

They named a tunnel after him, you know. The *Robin Williams* now connects the Golden Gate Bridge to Marin County. It has a rainbow border.

Rufus, indeed, lived a long, happy fat cat life. He's nineteen now, old, frail, a sketch of himself, a whisper on the breeze. He's half my age. He's been with me half of my life.

Aaff, he says to me, *aaff.*

Let me go.

Is that what he's saying? *Let me go?*

Hey, is what it actually seems. *Hey, I'm here. (I know because I hurt.) I'm here. I hurt. I'm here.*

Aaff, his grand barbaric yawp.

Robin writes on the blackboard, *I sound my barbaric yawp over the rooftops of the world,* and moves us all.

I have a friend who wouldn't allow her daughters to watch the Muppets but then they watched *Pet Cemetery.* This segue is to consider the question of continued life at what cost, not necessarily to critique mystifying parenting choices but.

She would agree with Wilhelm Grimm, violence is okay, risqué is not. As each fresh installment of the brothers' collection became less bawdy and much gorier at Wilhelm's insistence.

They're not authors, the Grimm brothers, but collectors, shapers. They gathered these folk and fairy tales from the grandmothers, then, yes, they wrote them down, but with a difference.

Horror movies are a kind of layman's philosophy. A safe space for people who don't normally think about death to contemplate their end. Briefly, though. So they can feel aroused at the reminder that they're not dead.

Pet Cemetery strikes me as very Christian.

Whereas the early Muppets are fairly subversive. I do see this.

Remember, Genie can't bring people back from the dead, it's not pretty, and he doesn't like doing it.

So, he can, in other words, but won't. Just like he won't kill anybody. This is why he makes Jafar a genie: immortal, a slave, forever stuck with Iago.

Men should be what they seem, Shakespeare's Iago says.

And Jafar is a slave to his desires.

But surely, Genie *could* put a stopper on death. Or make someone fall in love, alter their memories, flood them with oxytocin, serotonin, and dopamine. He could, but he won't.

Surely, there are other jinn who lack Genie's ethics. They are demons, after all, and most genie stories—like *Little Shop of Horrors*—are warnings. *Be careful what you wish for...*

I watched *Little Shop of Horrors* incessantly as a kid, which worried my parents, but it's literally Frank Oz collaborating with Alan Menken, the man responsible for *Aladdin*'s music.

Poof What do you need? *Poof* What do you need? *Poof* What do you need?

O god, let me keep Rufus until the end.

My dæmon, my animus, my familiar.

You must go on. I can't go on. I'll go on.

Robin Williams once played Estragon opposite Steve Martin's Vladimir in a staging of *Waiting for Godot*. Martin described Robin's Estragon as vulnerable and hurt.

Steve Martin, whom Disney producers also asked to play Genie.

I don't play down to kids, I play to them, Robin said.

Thinking of Sylvia Plath feeding her children just before she stuck her head in the oven, how she kissed them and locked their door. Trying to shield them as best she could.

It's hard to imagine Sylvia Plath's children behaving as erratically and immediately as mine do. Them crowding the bathroom, performing for the mirror, for the mommy, rambling on about noses on toes and eyeballs on fingertips. So alive, so wonderful.

Isn't this enough?

Sylvia Plath, who was married to a brutal man.

We never sleep trained, I couldn't handle it.

What a horrible way to go, putting one's head into an oven. I imagine she felt dizzy, faint. She used vertigo to end her life as though it were a sword.

Thinking of Tony Soprano fainting before the gabagool.

In *The Fisher King,* Robin falls back into the real after a true love's kiss. The Red Knight attacks, with his flaming plume, out to make sure Robin doesn't remember, chasing him so that he can't forget.

Robin qua Parry as in Percival. Here Robin as knight, not Merlin. However, Parry heals Jack's wound as much as Jack heals his. So, which one is the Fisher King? Which is the White Knight? Which the Fool? The answer bounces, it moves, it's alive.

Sometimes, when I look at the night sky, I get dizzy. As a kid someone once told me that at night God throws a blanket over the earth like a towel thrown over a birdcage and that the stars are the holes in the wool.

So we're all essentially in one blanket fort together.

Estragon: *What about hanging ourselves?*

Vladimir: *Hmm. It'd give us an erection.*

These two men are homeless, outsiders, but not alone. Very much aware of the other.

What even is acting?

Why does Robin feel like home? Like everything will be okay.

Niles Schwartz writes on Robin's homeless Parry: *[L]ong before Robin Williams committed suicide, I couldn't help but see a real person clawing away at himself, struggling to run away from what was inside.*

Schwartz is doing what I'm doing, claiming the actor, writing his way into an assumption.

I see me in you, therefore I see you.

I'm sorry, Robin. It's just that somehow through you I can write about (what isn't mine to say).

Schwartz also writes, *My memory of Robin Williams is that of our own generation's Knight of the Sorrowful Countenance, whose work here reached out through my own quandaries and brought me back to myself and those around me several times.*

Like some sad clown.

Alas poor Yorick! I knew him...

Here we revivify the actor, sculpting him back to life from the internet, as if he were a golem.

It's as though now Robin's a palimpsest, a scintillating compilation of his work and the cheugy memes people make of him.

Though Schwartz does go on to accurately say that the Holy Grail we seek is compassion, *that storytelling is itself compassion, a means of suffering with others while working through the morass of our own experiences.*

The Holy Grail as making art.

Not an inert thing, a process.

In the Tarot, the Grail holds the waters of imagination and feeling, a feminine suit and the pursuit of the masculine swords.

There's nothing trashy about romance. Romance is passion, imagination, it's beauty, Parry says to the girl of his new dreams.

But just before, propped up in a stapled suit, when he stands outside gathering the balls to ask her out, he tells Jack that he's scared. This knight is scared that something awful is about to happen. Something wonderful, something awful. They're tied for him, two sides of the same coin.

Something wonderful, something awful.

Because Parry is not Parry, he is Henry Sagan, professor, Arthurian myth scholar. When his wife was murdered, her brains blown all over his face, Henry splits, becomes Parry. So Parry is on a quest to save Henry, heal him enough so that he can love again.

This schizophrenic, *Psycho*-esque divided self protects, shields the one from the pain of the other.

But this process leaves biological traces.

Trauma leaves biological traces.

Ghosts in the nerves.

Like how if when your mother was very little and could never relax, how if she was always in fight or flight, always surviving, her fear then would corrode her DNA, your DNA, like Hexxus slime.

How some feelings, some reactions, you soon learn, are not your own.

Toxic love.

Some monsters punch the present from the past, some eat futures. Some snatch art from the minute jaws of toddler naps.

I'm happy. Why don't I feel safe?

I'm happy. Something's wrong.

Something wonderful, something awful.

Something old, something new, something borrowed, something blue.

Jane Austen: *We live at home, quiet, confined, and our feelings prey upon us.*

Ha ha ha, Grace Poole laughs.

The Birdcage bores me, gives me the ick. Confected gay coding, you can feel its inauthenticity.

Any character other than himself that he inhabits, really.

Robin tones down his Robinness when he's given a script. Best to let him go.

Watching him when he does, he can never stop moving, stop talking.

He can't fathom ever stopping because he knows if he stops, he dies.

One time, after Homer eats an unknown pill that he finds on the floor, he becomes afraid that if he stops talking, he'll die. I mean it like that.

The first time I took mushrooms I needed *The Simpsons* to avoid a psychic collapse.

It's all full circle.

The circle of life moves us all.

I stood on the sun-bleached pavement outside the funeral home and rebelled against the very idea that this would ever happen to me. Knowing full well that this will happen to one of us, my husband or me.

I go back and forth thinking about which one is worse, being inside the box or the one still outside of it.

Neither of us want to be buried, unless it's like with nothing but a burlap sack.

I could see us digging a hole in the backyard because it's a different kind of world and humans have regressed back to basics.

There's something romantic about being buried in the ground. Not the way we do it now though.

(Lately, it feels like we haven't gotten much of anything right.)

Gather ye rosebuds while ye may,
 Old Time is still a-flying;
And this same flower that smiles today
 Tomorrow will be dying.

Carpe diem, Robin whispers in his best ghost.

I want to bury Rufus in my parents' backyard. I tend to move a lot, they don't. I want to bury him at my parents' house so I can keep his bones close, but that's illegal in Illinois right now. I could defy the law, but if my parents ever wanted to move what then?

It's hard to imagine my parents outside of that house.

We are not made of this world, says our ego, that little window of consciousness. How lonesome, how terrifying. *How uncanny*, Heidegger says. For some, this alienating feeling is a comfort, proof of a God. For others, it's cause for a lorazepam.

Unheimlich in German translates to *uncanny*, but a literal translation would be *Unhomelike*.

The German word unheimlich *is obviously the opposite of* heimlich, heimisch, *meaning "familiar," "native," "belonging to the home"; and we are tempted to conclude that what is "uncanny" is frightening precisely because it is* not *known and familiar,* writes Freud. However, after much semantic analysis, his thesis is more that *unheimlich*, meaning the uncanny, is the revelation of what was private and concealed, what was hidden, not only from others but also from the self. In this way, the uncanny is the mark of the return of the repressed.

It's like a disguised presence, an imposter.

The pea under the mattress.

The term now commonly refers to animatronic CGI and its "uncanny valley."

Back now to the inverse: the phenomenon of celebrities whose digital presence is a comfort. That comfort becomes uncanny precisely because it's more familiar than the actual people in the photos on the walls of your home.

For Jacques Lacan, *Man finds his home in a point situated in the Other beyond the image of which we are made and this place represents the absence where we are.*

When home is alienated, alienating.

The unhomely (strange) is defined as homely (familiar): *The unheimlich is defined as heimlich. The Unheim is poised in the Heim.*

The hidden desires, Freud coos.

Including fantasies turned monstrous.

Is the uncanny best understood in representation?

In many fairy tales, the antagonist represents some psychological aspect of the hero that has to be killed.

In *The NeverEnding Story,* the Nothing is Sebastian's grief gone numb. Whereas the Black Hound of Hell after him—Gmork in this world—is the terror of death itself. As the Nothing consumes all of Fantasia, the Empress (the heart of the world) is dying. Sebastian, who thinks he's just a passive reader, learns he has to name her to save all of Fantasia and stop the Nothing. Meaning, Sebastian has to speak his grief if he wants to keep his imagination alive.

Reading is creation.

Aladdin has to resist the temptation of power, of corruption.

Choose love, not ego, no matter how snazzy the trappings may be.

With Jafar as Aladdin's foil, his three wishes mirror Aladdin's suppressed desires. Jafar wishes to rule, to enslave, and to become a god. To get what he wants with little effort. He desires to become corrupted, to fuse with force.

Think of what Aladdin has to go through for a loaf of bread. Nothing is easy for him.

Even after he endures a small sea of troubles to steal the bread, he gives it to two even hungrier children. The magic of this gift transforms the contraband into property—the orphans eat justly and Aladdin ceases to be a thief.

Aladdin makes a choice, he wants all that Jafar asks for, but with a distinction. He only truly wants power over himself. He wants to be master of his own destiny. He isn't even comfortable with Genie as a genie. He uses one wish to get respectable access into the palace; his next is made subconsciously—he was drowning, and though this presented an ethical quandary, Genie unwaveringly felt he *knew* Aladdin's will to live, thus, feels comfortable wishing on his behalf; and for his third wish, Aladdin ungenies Genie. Through this wish, he unshackles Genie from his obligation, his servitude. Meaning, Aladdin is a "thief" who resists temptation, the *Diamond in the Rough.*

You see, Genie didn't want to be found, and the Cave of Wonders was on his side.

And if Jafar represents Aladdin's evil foil, then we are to understand that this is the internal battle he is secretly fighting.

If Aladdin were to somehow uncover this revelation, the disembodied truth and untruth of it would strike as uncanny.

What if your battle is simply between choosing something over nothing?

I'm the janitor of God, Parry says.

Par•ry: to avoid, evade; to ward off a weapon or blow (the Red Knight/trauma).

Godot is God, of course.

Nothing happens, nobody comes, nobody goes, it's awful!

When my daughter asked me what happens to us when we die, I told her I didn't know, but that I heard we become stars. She liked that idea, us shining up there together.

Her dreams will take flight one day, away from me.

She'll get her sea legs and walk out of the mother waters to become a grown-up.

She will learn what it means to carry this self with her like a lantern, as she makes her way through life's desolate snow storms.

Indeed, the great Leonardo (da Vinci) remained like a child for the whole of his life in more than one way. It is said that all great men are bound to retain some infantile part. Even as an adult he continued to play, and this was another reason why he often appeared

uncanny and incomprehensible to his contemporaries.
Freud.

To me, Robin Williams was a star among stars, like Madonna, Princess Diana, or Kermit.

His voice felt like gravity, so familiar, so anchored.

Like a father or a lover.

I read an article about him recently. They always seem to make the rounds, new information about what a good person he was. (And surely my algorithms are tipped toward the man, given.) This article talked about his depression filming *Night at the Museum*. Everyone was on their phones. Here they were in the Smithsonian by themselves, at night, with him, and they were all on their devices. Some young actor put down his phone and walked over to him in front of the Rosetta Stone. They exchanged some words about it, some what has this world become words.

This is how I know he was sad about it, this actor who stopped to ask, and then the internet knows that there are all of these people who think of Robin as family, who will click and sigh and for a moment, dream of better things. Inspiration as commodity. And it works, for an instant. Then there's another thing, then another. Morsels, but the flavor changes too fast. Because the internet is relentless. (Like Beckett.)

So you simultaneously feel inspired and alienated.

The joy in running through the Smithsonian at night with Robin Williams though.

The *jouissance* of running around a museum late at night with any lover. Shipwrecked inside museums, malls, schools, when no one else is there. Significant liminal spaces frozen in time. Is there a better setting? No, there is not. The magic in the mundane.

As an editor, I debated here on using *joy* again or *jouissance*. But what I want to say is *jouissance féminine* to talk about the feminine desire for the perfect setting.

To mean rapture. To mean *explosion, diffusion, effervescence, abundance.* I mean *limitless*. (Hélène Cixous)

Though treated that way, a fantasy and a fairy tale are not the same thing.

My forever migraines shipwreck my daughter and me. Fairy tales help us through storms. They help me parent, they get my daughter to sit. We choose the stories based on what she's emotionally battling. There's a fairy tale for everything.

We don't have cable, we have DVDs. Little iridescent circles with pictures we place over them in a pretty book for my daughter to flip through. She likes to take out the pictures and line them all up for us to decide. Then we eliminate them one by one. The last one standing is the one we watch, but my daughter cheats like the dickens. We call this game, *Limination.*

We could stream, but it feels important to separate from the internet.

So we don't look at social media instead of the actual Rosetta Stone.

And still, it's like a shadow on us all the time.

La Nausée.

Scattered stream of references, one good for every ten, Seth MacFarlane said of Robin. He didn't get it, his art, his *joie de vivre.* Which shouldn't be surprising. You have to not have it all figured out.

But there is something to that, one good for every ten.

But that one changes from person to person, peer group to peer group. I used to watch *The Simpsons* at a dive bar in Iowa. It was fascinating to see the different tables erupt with laughter at the different jokes. I used to judge them on their preferences, I used to make whole swaths of assumptions. It's like more than anything else friendships are made through our senses of humor.

Death to Smoochy was his last movie that I think of as mine. He wore crazy well.

Estragon: *We're all born mad. Some remain so.*

Robin: *You've got to be crazy... Because what is reality?... You've got to be crazy. It's too late to be sane. Too late. You've got to go full tilt bozo. Because you're only given a little spark of madness. If you lose that, you're nothing. Don't—from me to you—don't ever lose that 'cause it keeps you alive. Because if you lose that...* then he makes a noise like *pshhh*. Like death.

Rufus's face feels like my face. His death is impossible.

Home. Home is a place of perfect belonging, wholeness. Home is an instinct, a yearning that has never, ever been satisfied, that can never be eradicated... Dodie Bellamy writes of her mother.

This is not a grief memoir.

Besides, autotheory is not memoir.

As a kid my favorite plushie—the loudmouth protagonist for years—was a stuffed magenta rhino with yellow ears. She had her own talk show. My brother loved it. Her name was Puffy.

Smoochy the Rhino has Puffy's exact same color scheme.

Is that uncanny?

A metaphor for anything?

The witch in me is a sucker for a metaphor.

For coincidences.

For meaning.

We also call Rufus, Sir Beef Wellington. Tubs, too, my hopeless Hufflepuff with his great round belly and his old man chirrups. He was born inside the insanity of my first apartment on a zigzagged blanket my great aunt had knit. Its color scheme looks like an autumn sunset. This was my attempt to feel some kin to ancestry.

I try to give him the birth blanket now. He looks at me, irritated, *Why are you giving this to me?*

These metaphors have no homes, they're homeless. I hug that old ass blanket now and cry.

My dæmon, my animus, my familiar.

Who loves kitty? Robin asks in gay.

The entire set of *Popeye* had been built on an island off the southern coast of Italy. It's still there, abandoned, in ruins, just there. Like the husk of an idea. Buildings made to look like buildings, not spaces to live in. Just raw material in the shape of a memory of a house.

Dæmon not like the Devil, of course, but rather like an animus.

What I mean is, in Lyra's world, everyone has an externalization of their soul in the form of an animal dæmon. As a child this dæmon changes animal shapes to suit something they're doing or feeling. When they reach puberty their dæmon settles form into something symbolically *them*. (Philip Pullman. *His Dark Materials.)*

Like a spirit animal.

Though we've been kindly asked to not use that phrase, we're offered *familiar* instead.

Either way, a spirit animal is very different from both a familiar and Jung's animus, which is the unconscious masculine factor in a woman. (Anima would be the feminine factor in a man.)

In Disney fairy tales, this would be the princess's animal sidekick.

Rufus, a fat, dopey, love muffin kitty, that's my masculine spirit.

Belle's animus is not the chipped teacup. It's the Beast himself. The teacup is her latent desire for children, for domestic normalcy. The Beast is her fury with the boring and indifferent provincial life. He's her raging sex.

But how disappointing is the Beast when he becomes a man? Belle was catfished.

As a catfish, inside his mother's belly, I felt Rufus flutter and pop like popcorn. Baby liked when I kept my hand there, she liked the pressure, wanted relief from the creatures within.

Rufus's mother's name had been Baby.

The *creature*, that's how Mary Shelley referred to the fetus inside her womb.

And then later, the monster in *Frankenstein*.

Of her five children, only one survived to adulthood.

Her husband died young too.

They say she kept his heart in her writing desk wrapped in silk. It is said that she had to fight Lord Byron for it too.

Percy Shelley died at sea. Once he washed to shore, his friends burnt the body then and there on the beach. They each took a piece of him. They say Byron took his heart and wouldn't give it back.

Byron, stealer of hearts, left many children dadless across Europe.

A man is a dad is a fuck is a chicken, Lisa says to Daisy, to the one who got out of the mental institution. Susanna covers her ears with a pillow in fear and disgust of Lisa, Daisy, herself, the situation, but mostly at her competing desires to out somebody's secret, to expose their fear, *their* inner ids, the chaos, and yet maintain composure, propriety, and dignity, hers and Daisy's. These are the glue that keeps society together, and the grease that slicks the wheels of the turning cogs. Susanna knows the difference between kindness and truth, but she's ambivalent where her alliance falls. For her, there's composure and there is madness. (*Girl, Interrupted.* Susanna Kaysen.)

Lisa has the guts to say what she wants, to call Daisy a fatherfucker, to crack the veneer of illusion, of Daisy's permitted leave, her apartment, her wicker furniture. Daisy's rape helps Lisa sleep at night, it quells her jealousy and her anger that Daisy is considered sane while both she and Susanna are still prisoners. Of course Susanna thinks all this, but only writes it; she is a fence-sitter, powerless, stuck, impuissant, just as she is when confronted with Daisy's swinging corpse. She can't run from her death, but Lisa is already out the door.

As all the inmates are a shade of Susanna, in the end, Lisa and her righteous rage must be sacrificed in order for Susanna to feel better, to feel normal, to be sane.

But then she still writes.

For it is usually because she is in some sense imbued with interiority that the witch-monster-madwoman becomes so crucial an avatar of the writer's own self, Sandra Gilbert and Susan Gubar scratch onto some innermost part of me, saying what I already knew at eight. (*The Madwoman in The Attic: The Woman Writer and the Nineteenth-Century Literary Imagination*)

The womb as the ultimate safe space, the protected asylum, but.

Now, Rufus wants me to hold his belly, just like his mother did. To ease the tension he's fighting. These death gurgles, they're farts. He smells terrible, but it comes to be what I smell when I relax because when I am in bed, he is there with me.

Julia Kristeva: *A wound with blood and pus, or the sickly, acrid smell of sweat, of decay, does not* signify *death. In the presence of signified death—a flat encephalograph, for instance—I would understand, react, or accept. No, as in true theater, without makeup or masks, refuse and corpses show me what I permanently thrust aside in order to live. These body fluids, this defilement, this shit are what life withstands, hardly and with difficulty, on the part of death. There, I am at the border of my condition as a living being.*

Shit is the border of our condition as a living being.

Talking about Kristeva, Dodie Bellamy writes, *Bodily emissions point up our mortality, our impending thingness.*

The corpse is the thing wherein I will catch the concept of the self.

The King of Everything bellows: *Please, please! Noooo! I don't want any more bodily functions!*

Yes, take my migraines!

O, that this too too solid flesh would melt Thaw and resolve itself into a dew!

Do I wish to be without a border though?

It's the real moments you miss the most, Robin says in *Goodwill Hunting,* talking about his dead wife's farts. *Those real moments are the ones that make you feel less alone at night.*

My mother revolves around rearranging furniture, repainting, redecorating. She never thinks the house is good enough, never just right enough, never done.

This is her madness.

Mine is in here. Kind of.

You see, this is both my story and not my story.

We all need a spark of madness.

Suzanne Scanlon writes of Kristeva: *[She] took seriously the link between reading and feeling. Identification. And not in a simple saccharine way, or a public service announcement where reading is unequivocally good. Rather, she acknowledged the risk and danger of it.*

And you know, danger is sexy.

Has it never happened, Kate Briggs writes that Barthes once asked, *as you were reading a book that you kept stopping as you read, not because you weren't interested, but because you were: because of a flow of ideas, stimuli, associations.*

You're jealous of that piece of writing, but no, not jealous, bewitched and hungry, you want to consume the mind, body, and soul of it.

To write is to want to rewrite, Barthes again. (Barthes forever.)

Associations, stimuli, a flow of ideas.

To be so moved while reading, to be transported, *stimulated,* that the sublime process of inspiration was almost painful, but delicious, like a crush, consuming the reader/writer with desire and lack.

A spark of madness.

Transfixed, possessed, the desire to write stems from the desire to consume (books, sentences, art) and possess in turn.

To see this process—the chain links—in an artist is magic, is pedestrian.

Watching *My Little Pony: Friendship is Magic* we see that Nightmare Moon is Maleficent, she trots across the screen celebrating Aurora's birth. Queen Chrysalis is Ursula, watch her sing in the mirror. King Sombre is the Horned King from *The Black Cauldron*. I couldn't place the chimera Discord though. I decided *Alice in Wonderland*. Because of his aesthetic, because I was distracted by his direct lineage to Q from *Star Trek*, and because he's so redeemed, he's inner circle now. He and his chaotic devil energy seem to belong in Carroll's upside-down math playground. But that wasn't right.

So Discord remained orphaned to me, forced.

Watching *Aladdin*, as Genie poofs in and out of personas, my daughter said, *He's like Discord!* Her brain works like mine, like Robin's, in references, in analogy. Genie, for all intents and purposes, functions exactly like Discord. She found his egg. I was so proud.

Except Discord isn't a slave.

But he did need a friend.

So did Genie.

(We all do.)

When Mumble approaches Lovelace the Guru penguin for advice, he says, *Go forth and multiply.* Then we hear lady penguins moan in the background, so he says, *Come to think of it, why don't we all go forth... and multiply?*

Foghorn Leghorn meets Barry White, Robin said of Lovelace. (*Happy Feet*)

Robin Williams recorded over sixteen hours of raw material for *Aladdin*. Disney likes to say they just let him run wild.

There is reference to this a lot with Robin, letting him run wild. As though he were a beast.

Something animal about him. Feral.

The way he sweats when he performs, the dozens of water bottles surrounding him, his intense body hair.

Hairiness indicates masculinity, this is why women remove it.

We have been expected to lie with our bodies: to bleach, redden, unkink or curl our hair, pluck eyebrows, shave armpits, wear padding in various places or lace ourselves, take little steps, glaze finger and toe nails, wear clothes that emphasized our helplessness, Adrienne Rich writes. (*Women and Honor: Some Notes on Lying*)

I am the oldest cousin on my mother's side. When the adults drank and played cards sitting around dining room tables, they would laugh and smoke as we schemed ways to steal snacks and coins. The second eldest cousin was also a girl, the rest were boys. We were the regents and they were our soldiers, we sent them into the field then we parsed the spoils. It was our job to watch over them, the five boys. We watched a lot of movies when we all got together. It's how children understand time. An hour is too abstract, but when *The Lion King* is over makes sense.

An hour is a sequence of numbers, a story is a lifetime.

It is not uncommon for children to live several lifetimes in one day.

I didn't know this uncle, the one who died. He wasn't around the time period when I was around. That was a different uncle. My aunt's husband shape-shifted from one form to another, the first shape being someone who is now effectively no longer my uncle. Which may be weird, except, I didn't know him either. It would be weirder to pass him on the street, recognize him, and say, *Hi, Uncle Dave.* He would be like, *Who are you?*

One night a man broke into my apartment while I was sleeping and sexually assaulted me. When I screamed, he left. In a way, I'm very lucky.

My aunt called me the next morning to tell me her story. She had never called me before and has since never called me again.

The second uncle shape had a mustache and a good laugh, like a machine gun laugh. I think he liked to chew gum. Maybe he smoked. He seemed amused enough, affable. I don't think he's ever said anything to me besides, *Hi, Cath*.

One time, around him, I answered my father with, *I'm not into suffering*. He laughed real hard at that. I liked him enough.

Actually, that might have been my other uncle-in-law.

Robin Williams had a charming laugh too. For a pinprick of a second you can see when the joke breaks through the crust of his persona and touches his inmost self, you can see authenticity move across his face. It's beautiful.

There's a singular kind of pride or allure I feel when making someone funny laugh.

I imagine it's similar to the feelings other girls have when they dance, the way they feel they look when they contort their bodies into a honey trap. It's not that I don't also use my body to attract men, just never by dancing. I have never not looked dumb dancing.

Maybe I'm just too uptight.

Who here hasn't rewound that part in *Aladdin* when he's all Romeo at her window? You have to yell at everyone in the room to be very quiet, and the sound has to be all the way up. *Good kitty,* Aladdin will say. Then, wait for it... *Take off your clothes!*

Like the priest's boner in *The Little Mermaid*, or *Sex* written in *The Lion King* clouds, or the big golden dick tucked into King Triton's castle on clam shell. On the DVDs now, all of that stuff is gone. Such were the legends of VHS.

Like how Han doesn't shoot first. As though he isn't a scoundrel.

There is an intimacy in experiencing someone else's wit, you can feel the thrust of it.

Finding out Robin Williams had drug problems made me love him even more.

But I was unimpressed with how much my mom's family drank.

Alcoholics, Robin says, *are all like assholes: they can't wait to shit on everybody.*

37

I liked the impression he gave of someone's reaction to him on drugs. The kid, his dealer—so ecstatic to be hanging out with Robin fucking Williams—looks over at him and is surprised, he says, *You're really boring when you're on cocaine.* It's a self-deprecating joke, obviously. One, I think, that hints at that inmost self, Robin the Creator.

I was going to say, *true self.* But what do I know?

Maybe he's thinking about fields of landmines.

But you know what I mean, right?

Robin on sobriety: *The thing that matters are others. Way beyond yourself. Self goes away. Ego? Bye bye.*

What they first thought was Parkinson's was actually a kind of dementia. As the Lewy bodies colonized his brain, he felt this self slipping. That he couldn't improv anymore, that he couldn't really go wild. Insecure, mad, spiraling. Embarrassed even of his final performances, asking of the takes, *Are they even usable?*

The doctor said he had one of the worst cases he'd ever seen, and that it was his brilliance that enabled him to endure far longer than they thought possible.

Robin said that when he was on drugs, he stared out of windows a lot. Thinking about, one imagines, his act.

Did he do drugs to get lost inside his art? A way to never stop the ride?

Kin.

Shut up, I hear. *The author is dead.*

As is Robin and my uncle.

As soon my cat will be.

Wuthering Heights is a story about a house where a series of characters look out of windows and long for someone else.

Dying, Cathy looks out her window and longs for home, her real home. Her home now, Thrushcross Grange, is *unhomelike*, named it seems, after a yeast infection, an excuse to never have sex. Home is Wuthering Heights. Home is Heathcliff, her Other, her person, her Beast, her animus.

Trying not to feel homeless, looking out of windows is a lot like looking into screens.

You know what music is? It's God's little reminder that there's something else in this universe besides us. Harmonic connection between everything, even the stars, Robin says as Wizard, one of the rare villains he played.

When Robin did his time on *Inside the Actor's Studio*, he made an audience member laugh so hard the man busted a gut and had to be wheeled away in an ambulance.

Literally, this man's organ slipped through his muscle tissue.

That show was filmed inside my graduate school.

Coincidences, not all of them are meaningful.

The school used to be called The University in Exile. A much better name than The New School.

My parents are not alcoholics. This outcasted us with my mother's family in nearly imperceptible ways, accumulating to where I could no longer unsee it.

My father calls my mother Marilyn Munster. He loves her so much. Like awestruck love. Like she comes first forever and always kind of love.

This is no small feat, to choose yourself, to choose good, when everyone else is telling you no.

I feel more comfortable with my father's family, but that was all his mother. She's been dead for some time now. I have a lot of her things. A lot of paintings and sketches. She was the artist in the family. I remember drawing with her at her kitchen table with its PVC table cloth, church channel on the little tv, angel food cake on the counter.

I'm pretty sure she'd hate my writing. The impropriety of it, the foolishness of it, the vanity and obscenity of it. The frivolous art slut of it. I don't know.

With her last words to me she told me not to make my writing too weird.

Am I doing it right?

I found out after her death that once upon a time she loved someone she couldn't have and then gave their lovechild to someone else. I wish I had known about this, before.

I wish more adults in my life had been real people. Alas.

She was my confirmation sponsor, which is basically another godparent, which to me, was an empty ritual. I fought hard to not be confirmed. Alas, I was a minor.

Godparents, it is said, are to make sure you become a true worker for the Kingdom of Christ. My godparents are my mother's other sister and one of my father's brothers. I don't think I've ever spoken to either of them about the Kingdom of Christ. One is dead, the other hates me or doesn't think of me. I don't really care anymore, but I used to.

My husband and I didn't marry in a church either. We did it alone in our living room. That felt right, felt like ours.

For a while, my mother tried drinking with her widowed sister. She had a ball when she drank with that sister. The thrill of defying her migraines, I think. Of letting go, regressing.

For me it's no longer worth the headache.

Now, they're not talking again.

My mother accepts the headache to feel the joy, to forget their shared memories are frayed, connected by a live wire.

I haven't drank since I lived in that apartment on the train tracks. Sleeping, I could feel the train roaring out of my chest, then coming back in between my thighs. Train as lover.

Or maybe I birthed it, only to have it force its way back into my eye. Train as migraine.

I spent that ouroboros train year as a mistress. He wasn't married, but he had a girlfriend. He's married to her now though.

I loved him all the same.

That was when Rufus would wail at his empty bowl and pretend to faint from hunger. Painfully relatable, I fed him, so did my roommate. He gained six pounds in six months, ended up a twenty-six-pound tom.

We were both indulgent with our appetites that year, my animus and me.

When Anaïs Nin was two, her father's jilted lover—a servant he had seduced and then forgotten—left her and her baby brother to die in the middle of the railroad track. As a train approached, a brave signalman risked his life to push the carriage out of the way while he carried little Anaïs off in his arms. In her dairy she writes that this event remained in her memory.

Rufus loved pie. He would caterwaul at pies in the oven, scratching at the glass, longing to be with the pie. Rhubarb was our family pie, which feels like a Midwestern crest. To be sure, my father's mother's crest, not my mother's mother.

My mother's mother never did anything maternal like bake a pie, at least not near me. Of course, I can concede that she may be different outside of what I know, but that doesn't change her grandmother shape in my mind. Doesn't erase what I know.

On the tracks, Rufus was in love with the neighbor's cat, a black beauty named Mina Loy who lived in an apartment that Charlie Chaplin once lived in. Rufus sang opera to this posh kitty from the roof, I imagined to the tune of *Pagliacci*. *Minaaaaaaa, I loooove youuuuuuuu.* At least that's how I tell the story to my daughter who laughs and laughs.

Rufus the sad clown.

Mina Loy, who once said, *Poetry is prose bewitched, a music made of visual thoughts, the sound of an idea.*

Rufus's love went unrequited. A kind of *Pardon me, Miss Snooty Cat* scene that never progressed.

In *The Final Cut*, we live in a world where consciousness has a recording device embedded within. Robin plays an editor, cutting away the incriminating scenes from the newly dead's lifetapes. Solid meh, but what fun if this were written by a poet instead.

Trauma never feels real, it can't, it's too much of a surprise.

After that man broke into my apartment, my aunt called to see if I was alright. Shocked that she wanted to talk to me, that she cared, she really just wanted to crack open the egg of family. To tell me the things my mother hadn't. To attempt to get the horrible out of her body. Then like a ghost, she disappeared in a trail of smoke.

Estragon: *Don't let's do anything. It's safer.*

When the police came, they asked me if I had been drinking, then they left. They never found the guy who went around checking apartment doors in the morning, who ducked as I screamed so I couldn't clock his height, who had obviously done this before.

Don't let's do anything. It's safer.

If you were to read a transcript of Robin's act you would miss the essential tones he's calling, the visceral memories of audio/visual references he's recalling.

This joke about being drunk: *You're laying in bed and you feel like the scene from the movie* The Fly. *And you're going:* Help meee! Help meeeeeee! *The entire room is spinning like a roulette wheel:* Place your bets! Place your bets! *And there was the old toilet in the corner going:* Talk to me!

Each line has its own voice, effectively placing four personalities on stage.

Associations, stimuli, a flow of ideas.

Then, immediately it was on to the next set. It's like you could just change his channel and he became someone else.

Zero people were surprised he had a coke habit.

Abjection: a breakdown between what is the self and what is other.

At the height of himself, Disney and an indie cartoon company both had created children story characters inspired by, who were both translations, or rather, manifestations of his frenetic schtick.

To lure, Disney animated him as Genie performing his *Reality... What a Concept* album. Genie, uncanny in pencil, begins to lecture on schizophrenia when he sprouts another head that yells at him in a different voice, still his, but *othered*. They're not impressions, they're personas, characters. Characters in that rudimentary understanding of multiple personality disorder.

(Which is now called dissociative identity disorder.)

Having first promised himself to *FernGully: The Last Rainforest*, he felt accepting the role as Genie was adulterous. He ultimately acquiesced, but had *a couple of provisos, quid pro quos.* Namely, his voice or name could not be used to promote *Aladdin* or sell any of its merchandise in any way. Disney agreed then reneged because of course they did. Deeply believing in *FernGully*'s message, he didn't want Disney to eclipse it. But then Disney pulled an Ursula and said, *We own your voice, you cannot sing The Batty Rap.* To which Robin responded, *Fuck you,* and totally sang *The Batty Rap.* Disney then showed everyone whose bitch he was and used his character and voice *here, here, here, here, here, here, here, anywhere!*

Robin wouldn't talk to them for years, not until they apologized.

They eventually did apologize and we all got *Flubber*.

Flying Rubber, an *innovative but unstable substance*, another play on his schtick. The scientist he played was calm, the flubber represented his suppressed madness.

Disney's first attempt at an apology came in the shape of an original Picasso: a self-portrait of the artist dressed as Vincent Van Gogh. Robin was like, *WTF? No.*

But really, in the vein of his technique, it's a nice analogy: impersonation as high art.

The painting was still in his basement the day he died.

The violation that must have felt like though, a corporation using your voice like that.

Another of Robin's quid pro quos was that if he were to star, the studio was required to hire several homeless people alongside. This was a common rider clause of his.

They say he used to don disguises and hang out with hobos in alleys, under bridges all the time.

They were his people, those who had shit luck.

It seemed as though he didn't feel like a celebrity, just very popular at a party past its prime.

There are loads of stories of people running into him in all sorts of common spaces. Weirdly, he would run into the same strangers twice, in different cities too. They say he would remember them.

They all talk about how delightful he was.

He met his third wife, his widow, at an Apple store. He was wearing a camouflage shirt.

How's the camo working out for you? she had asked him.

Not too good, he said, *You found me.*

Batty Koda, the deuteragonist fruit bat from *FernGully,* escapes from a biology laboratory just outside the forest. He's traumatized, schizophrenic. The doctors had left electric shock wires through his poor head and wings. If someone bops the wires, his personality changes. He's a sidekick, a friend. Stupid, funny, along for the ride. He's also a mentor, Krysta's animus, her superego suspicion and fears manifest. With his overactive nervous system, Batty Koda screams warnings to protect her from all things scary, especially human boys. Batty does not want her to grow up. (*Don't let's do anything. It's safer.*)

Just like Abu and Aladdin.

Normally, Robin plays the opposite and encourages maturity (through immaturity).

Batty is afraid, stuck in his trauma from the humans, the same humans who are destroying the forest. It's up to Krysta to change their mind, to stop all this pointless destruction. She does this through love.

Nuts to Batty, Krysta can't let her star-crossed love leave without telling him. Finally, she feels that latent femme magic blossom into the fertile queen she is. Her grand flower popping finale is about as symbolically obvious as the train in *Casablanca*.

Fairies, whose stories are those of the Mother Goddess, are also sluts. It is known.

Fairy tales are about money, marriage, and men. They are the maps and manuals that are passed down from mothers and grandmothers to help [their daughters] survive, writes Marina Warner.

The grandmothers told their wee kin these fairy tales to keep them alive, to keep them cautious, and to keep them breeding. Even though.

That's why there's a suspicious number of absent mothers. Because so often women wouldn't make it.

There is so much ancestral trauma in all of us.

Mapped in our DNA are the horrors of our great, great grandmothers' memories.

I definitely would've died in the birthing bed without the same technology that made the whole experience awful.

In *Tangled,* Pascal is Rapunzel's chameleon animus. He's cunning, cynical, ambitious. Sick of Mother Gothel, sick of being kept in a tower, he kills her. Trips her very old ass out the window to her death, poofing her into a pile of dust. Rapunzel wanted to kill her "mother," but she didn't, she suppresses that, because she's good. Everyone loves this little drop of sunshine and her silly floating lights dream, her longing for home, to feel *home.*

Something in her soul felt off. *Unheimlich.* She had to leave, but in order to do that she had to break the rules. So she chooses a bad boy thief with a sexy smolder, as well as an army of ruffians she's enchanted, to represent, to ensure the lengths she's willing to go to get home. Rapunzel fights dirty, she's scrappy and resourceful. And there's a shade of a murderer inside her.

Inside us all, fairy tales warn.

It's the monsters in our basement, our beasts and minotaurs.

They serve us, they keep us safe.

Remember me, they whisper.

In *The Poetics of Space,* Gaston Bacchelard writes: *A house constitutes a body of images that give mankind proofs or illusions of stability.*

If the house is a vertical being, the proof is the dichotomy between the attic and the cellar. The rationality of the attic. The irrationality of the cellar.

This housebody feels like a person, helping validate my *personhood* as a thing too, something safe and real, not imaginary and reflective.

The cellar then becomes buried madness, welled-in tragedy, Bacchelard writes.

Think of the Navidson Record.

But then again, for me and Jane Eyre, there are madwomen in our attics.

Mother Gothel is not a foil to Rapunzel, but to her real mother.

Another good mother versus bad mother story. Like *Snow White, Cinderella,* or *Coraline.*

When children realize their mother is not just an extension of themselves, but her own person, they revolt. The child cannot cope with the mother deserting her, scolding her, not feeding her the second she demands, not moving the toy around in that exact way she saw it in her head. When the child realizes that the womb party is over, that she is on her own, suddenly the mother person is not to be trusted. What baby wants is now frequently at odds with what the mother wants. Baby's brain adapts, makes due, says no. Often then, the child others her mother, splits her in two.

This is, of course, much intensified in children with abusive mothers.

The Ego is incapable of splitting the object—internal and external—without a corresponding splitting taking place within the Ego, writes Melanie Klein.

This schizoid split is a trauma response. The victim bottles part of her past, she then holds the unbearable feelings inside another past self, deep inside her muscle memories. Repression protects the ego, but resurfaces later in nightmares, addiction, depression, severe anxiety, etc.

Last night watching *Neon Genesis Evangelion,* I broke down and wept. When the characters pilot the Eva and their psyches split, multiply, and fracture, they lose sight of who they are and expose the vacuous space where the self is assembled.

It's nauseating to think of all the Cathys, the ones inside all the minds of everyone I know.

The Cathys from lifetimes ago. The versions I've forgotten, buried.

Before Peter remembers he's Pan, Robin drips, droops depression. *Hook*, like *Mary Poppins*, warns against repressing your joy. Tells you when you're depressed to go find your inner child and fly a kite with them, to throw food and run around with them, to eat junk and watch cartoons with them.

Even though he'd said that he knew depression, Robin did not kill himself because he was depressed.

You've seen the memes: *I think the saddest people always try their hardest to make people happy because they know what it's like to feel absolutely worthless and they don't want anyone else to feel like that.*

This is a Robin someone (AI?) has created for the masses. A Robin in someone's head who only thought himself worthless, and therefore, joked incessantly, as a gift, in an attempt to make everyone around him feel as though they had worth.

Laughing, at best, would be a distraction from worthlessness. Hardly seems like a solution to the problem, laughing.

By meme, I mean an insight with an analogy, or an image juxtaposed with food for thought, an attempt at quick relatability.

Lacan's mirror stage gives rise to an aggressive tension between the subject and its mirror image. How the baby sees her body whole in the mirror, but doesn't yet feel in control of all of it herself. So she others her image and begins to think of herself as fragmented. The baby thus feels a rivalry with her own image, pissed that it's better than her, just like her perceived omnipotent mother.

No one has ever gotten as angry at me as my daughter. Furious that my body, my will is not hers.

There's only one thing babies want from their mothers, my best friend says, *total submission.*

Hook, like *Mary Poppins,* guilts parents into being present.

My mom has two sisters and two half-brothers, though one has passed. She's the oldest, her mother had her at fifteen. When I was younger, I found this fact so interesting because it was the exact opposite of any option I was given.

My mother tended to all her siblings, especially the boys. Her mother went out.

I don't think much of my mother's mother. She was my age now when she became a grandmother. We never had any kind of relationship. No birthday calls or care beyond forced doorway kisses.

But that's not why I don't like her.

The other grandkids don't mind, or don't know. So I'm the family's rage.

She should've done more, done something.

Children deserve better.

She won't apologize either. For any of it.

We don't speak anymore, not really. My skin crawls when she talks to my kid or likes a photo my mom posts.

Some nights I dream of yelling and yelling at her. Those nights I wake with a headache.

Rufus's mother was a teenager when she had her babies, she was not even a year old. When nursing, if I left the room, Baby would abruptly stand up and let her babies drop to the floor like cracked eggs. She would follow me to the bathroom or the kitchen, meowing and meowing: *Don't leave me.*

Don't leave me.

You found me.

Eventually, one of my landlords found out I was harboring too many cats and I could no longer keep them. My friends took the other kittens and my parents took Rufus. I kept Baby, but quickly, sadly, she went insane. My dad paid five hundred dollars for Rufus's mother to live out the rest of her life in an old lady's mansion, a fancy no-kill shelter.

A charming Victorian mansion full of art and cats.

I know this sounds like a lie, but my father isn't like that.

I like to think of her as a madcat living her best life in some gothic attic somewhere.

Ha ha ha, Grace Poole laughs.

Motherhood made her insane. The poor thing went into heat at six months. She didn't like her kittens, despised baby Rufus most of all. He looked most like his father, and she had nothing but burning hatred for the father. Toms have spiky penises, I assumed that was why. They also can't pull out until they finish. It's painful, but it's the only palliative to the wild, desperate ache of estrus.

The spiky dick, the one full of regret, that's a metaphor.

So is motherhood causing madness.

So teenage catmom stuffed baby Rufus into a boot where he'd cry and cry the tiniest, squeakiest abandoned kitten wail. *Not this one,* her eyes would say to me when I rescued him. He was two days old, she did this for weeks. She didn't do this with the three others, only Rufus.

The vet said this would happen, she said she was too young, that she would go crazy, that she could possibly eat them. But there are no kitty abortions.

Mother knows best, Rapunzel's other mother sings. *Listen to your mother, it's a scary world out there. Mother knows best, one way or another, something will go wrong, I swear. Ruffians, thugs, poison ivy, quicksand, cannibals, and snakes, the plague. Also, large bugs, men with pointy teeth, and... Stop, no more, you'll just upset me!*

My mother sings the same song.

They're not wrong, these scared mothers. The world is terrible.

Rufus's mother, how she rebuffed him, laid the path for the rest of the mollies in his life. How they all spurned him too, from Gidget to Mina to Joy Division.

I am not projecting.

The first illusion it is to your interest to demolish is the division of women into two classes, the mistress, and the mother, every well-balanced and developed woman knows that is not true, writes Mina Loy in her *Feminist Manifesto.*

Because of course, there is no rapable woman, despite what Henry Miller or *Sixteen Candles* says.

Jim Henson was cursed with fame, it robbed us of his art. Ever trying to assign other people to deal with his Muppets, he could only chase his visions in the cracks of his ever-shrinking time. His last movie was *Labyrinth*. I read in *The Goblins of Labyrinth* that Jareth signals the brooding romantic figures of the nineteenth century. Heathcliff in *Wuthering Heights* and Rochester from *Jane Eyre*. Austen's Darcy, too.

Why have tall, dark, and handsome, Robin asks, *when you can have short, furry, and funny?*

Wondering if all three of those authors also lusted after the Dane.

Now thinking of Robin Williams playing Osric in Kenneth Branagh's *Hamlet.*

Osric—whose function is to invite Prince Hamlet to his death—is a bit of comic relief before the final act. He's there on behalf of Polonius, seeking justice for the poor chap who thought he was in a romcom.

Robin Williams enters the scene and seeks justice for the funny.

Alas. Laughter always fades.

Osric's most famous for: *A hit, a very palpable hit.*

Dost thou know this waterfly? Hamlet whispers to Horatio as Osric approaches them.

Waterflies are insects that dance aimlessly to and fro over the surface of water.

Robin Williams moved like a waterfly, like poetry. All artifice. *I don't tell jokes*, he said, *I just use characters as a vehicle for me. But I seldom just talk as myself.*

His words crashed into one another like cars in a pile up, except not like that at all, like cars that almost crash into each other but instead float above and break out into choreographed musicals. His ideas never collided, they flowed like a river and its current. Like time, like consciousness. Immense forward momentum.

He reminds me of jazz music, or James Joyce, or the rush of drugs.

On drugs, everything seems so profound, so green.

Standup was a great survival mechanism. For me, that's a joy. That's jazz. That's what I have to do, Robin once said.

When you make art, you can become your art, you can hide behind your art.

I do voices, he said.

If this text were to truly embody Robin's style, his self-generating stream of impressions, it should read more like Djuna Barnes's *Nightwood*, where each chapter takes on the style of another.

It would be every paragraph, though, or line.

I love thinking of Djuna in her winter years writing in bed with a full face of makeup, dropping pages to the floor like cigarette ash. She did voices. I'm cutting and pasting and curating and doing so to conceal/reveal/conceal the stories that are not mine.

Going for a performative use of citation.

My plan was to never get married. I was going to be an art monster instead. Women almost never become art monsters because art monsters only concern themselves with art, never mundane things. Nabokov didn't even fold his own umbrella. Vera licked his stamps for him, Jenny Offill writes.

Rosemary for remembrance, for the teenage art monster inside of me. Who smokes and barks: *Why aren't we writing?!*

What do you want to be in the world? I mean the whole world. What do you want to be? Close your eyes and think about that, Wizard Robin asks us.

Writing.

The mental agility, Marc Maron said of Robin. *An electric, shining piece of humanity... that was known to depart on riffs that almost essentially enabled him to avoid himself in a lot of ways.*

Once Robin was asked what he's afraid of: *I guess I fear my consciousness becoming not just dull, but a rock, I couldn't spark.*

After one of his epic late-night phone calls with Robin, Billy Crystal had said that when they hung up, they were exhausted, *like two jazz musicians who just got new horns.*

Lisa Simpson describes jazz as listening to the notes the saxophonist doesn't play.

That saxophonist's death hit hard for Lisa. He felt like family, another father. An art father.

I have art mothers: Jane, Emily, Charlotte, Virginia, Anaïs, Sylvia, Hélène, Margaret, Lidia.

Once upon a time I thought my biological grandfather was dead and Italian. When I watched *The Sopranos* I thought, *These, these are my people,* as I made spaghetti from cans of tomatoes and boxed noodles.

We found out later that my mother's father was alive and Hungarian. Then nope, Italian again. *Marone!*

Either way he's dead now.

Marone is short for Madonna, btw.

But I have no people.

Unhomelike.

By the time I was fifteen I stopped attending the family parties.

My mother's adopted father is Irish. So I thought I was Chicago South Side Irish for a while too.

Though inevitably I was bullied out of that neighborhood, out of the church, and driven to the pastel Westside.

I do feel like a Northerner, whatever that means.

That I'm a Stark, I guess.

Maybe a hobbit.

Hogwarts could be home. That feels right. Reading, falling in love in Ravenclaw Tower.

Either way, I now make my gravy with actual tomatoes.

I'm trying to be the kind of adult who tends a garden. Every good witch grows her own food.

Robin really, really wanted to play Hagrid in the movies, but they had a Brits only policy.

Like Hagrid's hut, Robin's humor lives on the edges. (See what I did there?)

What I mean is, the edges of what's offensive.

That was a statement for the beforetimes. Offensive now has no edges, it's more rhizomatic.

So, of course, *Mrs. Doubtfire* is transphobic.

A straight man cross-dressing to serve his own interests, no doubt, felt more Shakespearian to him. He was not in the business of making anyone feel bad.

Even though, sure, many times he inadvertently did.

People used to be comfortable seeing themselves in caricature. We all embraced the carnivalesque a bit more. Understood our small role in things. After all, caricature was a rainbow bridge to our current era.

I do still like *Mrs. Doubtfire* though.

I quoted Heidegger above too. And Bettelheim below.

But I won't talk about how much I love *Annie Hall*.

...And then they were upon her.

I saw a meme that said when you ask white people their nationality, they give you a math equation. How silly to compare stats, as it were, with your friends, turn yourself into a baseball card. I assumed everyone else was full of shit too when I threw out numbers like 42% Irish, 28% Italian, 9% French, 5% English, Scottish, and Welsh. It didn't matter if it added to one hundred.

Those are vaguely my stats, though, just maybe add some Hungarian and Polish. I don't know.

After the World Wars do these things still matter?

An impression of a Scotsman inventing golf: *Right near the end, I'll put a flat piece with a little flag to give you fucking hope, but then I'll put a pool and a sandbox to fuck with your ball again!*

That bit in its entirety is so sculpted, so written. He took his time to write it.

Just as it took the CGI people months to animate the shiny jello flubber bits when he went rogue in a scene.

Rosemary for all the artists forced to pivot to computer art.

I've heard there's a secret version of *Mrs. Doubtfire* locked away somewhere, an adult version, because Robin would only read the original script if they would also record him, let him ad lib inside the character.

So, unscripted but still sculpted.

I imagine him in bed, looking out his window, thinking of jokes, what makes a joke, cracking the comedic fault lines inside tragic nuts.

Did he ever write anything down?

It angers me, art being locked away.

Art belongs to everyone, imho.

My therapist says I live too much in fantasy.

Eh, a benign coping mechanism, I say. It could be so much worse, given my ancestry.

But I'm either awed by beauty or in the throes of nihilistic despair. I don't seem to have much of an in-between.

How pitifully emo of me.

It's not wrong though.

Reality is a fantasy, man.

Male fantasy is seen as something that can create reality, whereas female fantasy is regarded as pure escape. bell hooks.

Friedrich Nietzsche says that nihilism isn't a choice, that it suddenly just is. That it *stands at the door.*

Whence comes this uncanniest of all guests? Nietzsche writes. For me, it stands at the door of banality.

I didn't know my father's father, he died of cancer when my dad was in high school. He met my mother shortly after.

This cancer sits in my DNA soup, gnawing at my guts. He smoked a lot, apparently. So did I, but I quit in my twenties, cheating occasionally into my thirties. The hypochondria became too much.

I sure miss them though.

I'll forever be a smoker who doesn't smoke.

Real ballsy comedy is deeper than anger, Robin once said, *beneath the anger is the fear.*

Fear is also a kind of courage, Hélène Cixous writes.

Come, fly with me, gatina, the Brazilian helicopter pilot from *Inside-Out* (the mother's fantasy) says.

Except fly as in Cixous's *voler*: *To fly/steal is woman's gesture, to steal into language to make it fly.*

Come, write with me, gatina.

Mulan is only an honorary princess. So not at all a princess, and yet. She grabbed the kept daughter trope and twisted the narrative into a hero's journey. As soon as she did that, the story birthed her a tiny, mouthy dragon animus.

Fated to be a concubine, the real Mulan killed herself instead.

My daughter's art teacher was one of Mushu's animators. Now he zoom calls my daughter and a handful of lucky kids.

Hypochondria runs in the family. (Of course it does.) My mother, her mother, and me, we each have our own flavors of the absurd affliction. My daughter has it too.

I'm fine. Something must be wrong.

Always expecting something to hit you.

Even though I tried to hide it from my daughter, of course, I couldn't.

Of madness and wisdom, Cixous again, *one is the other, just as beauty is the beast.*

My daughter brought a "time-turner" to show and tell, an old brass, broken clock necklace charm. She told the kids once she gets it working, she could relive any memory.

What fairy stories really tell you is that inside of love is grief. That grief is love turned inside out.

One is the other. *Just as beauty is the beast.*

Three times the vet told me that Rufus was dying, then each of his three weird symptoms just became part of the new normal.

When my daughter was a toddler, he had a most inconvenient obsession with milk. Battles, all day, my daughter and cat. Neither liked to share me, or the milk.

When I nursed her, they would both sleep on me.

Turns out he was severely diabetic.

Now, my daughter thinks Rufus is gross with his old man farts and his puke and the way he smells like New York City. She is not wrong. He is a gross cat.

My atheism is like a black eye on my Catholic family. We don't really talk about it.

Metaphors, analogies.

Catholic symbols and iconography decorate my home all the same.

Catholics are my people, I guess.

Does that count for anything?

Same myths in my daughter's life, just not taught as Truth.

Hagrid, I don't know, but imagine Robin actually as Merlin. An older, wizened, more subdued Robin. Imagine, subtle lessons about kingly duties braided against Arthur's role as the bridge between paganism and Christianity, between the Goddess and the God. Lots of swimming with the priestesses of Avalon and knightly tomfoolery. Courtly romance, holy relic quests, faith embroidered. A film—no, let's make it a miniseries—steeped in philosophy and magic. It's pretty to think about.

Gentlemen, open your books to page 21 of the introduction...

Throw away your stuffy introductions, teacher Robin says, *Poetry, beauty, romance, love, these are what we stay alive for.*

That scene is so saccharine, so inspiring.

But the kids gleefully destroying their books, I find it unnerving.

Like when characters trash a room. I don't like it.

It's the opposite of watching Merlin shrink his whole house into a carpet bag, books and all.

That's the Virgo in me, my best friend would say.

Also, poetry isn't just about feeling, it's also about process and method, puzzles and keys. Introductions are helpful.

Albeit, the one they rip out is rather uninspired.

Still, those poor spines. The monstrous jagged pages. The orphaned poems.

And like the cat I have nine times to die. (Plath)

I thought Rufus was only on his sixth life. There was the pool, diabetes, that one time he ran between my father's legs and slept with the raccoons and coyotes. I know he's died of heartbreak thrice. What are the stories I don't know about?

Sad, scary creep Robin is not my preferred Robin. When he acts anything other than the good guy, my body rebels. It's uncomfortable, uncanny. They said he would be all goofy in between takes, he would be himself (as we know him), screwing up the actors' feelings towards him.

The public didn't like it much either, they missed the Mork of him.

But how exhausting to keep up.

That channel changing thing he does is very Morkish.

Alien communicating through bricolage and analogy because alienated. This I relate to.

That's how he was discovered, playing Mork on the street for the money people left in his hat.

To see him now as a meme for depression is depressing, both hollowed and homeless. And unfair, how he doesn't have a say. And given his track record on using his voice and image against his will...

How gross, to commodify the dead.

Am I guilty of this?

Revivifying his corpse to reify "his" brand.

They do this to Jim Henson too.

He didn't want his face, his voice selling anything. Wouldn't this include life?

He explicitly told everyone, bringing people back from the dead is not a pretty picture and he doesn't like doing it.

So Freud says the uncanny is not just something not of the home, it's when something's icky, something hidden and wrong inside the home is instead suddenly revealed.

A secret, then.

A disgusting one too, one that makes us uncomfortable.

Once it's revealed though, the secret then is no longer a secret.

But is it no longer uncanny?

Uncanny must have a shelf life.

Freud says that, *the feeling of something uncanny is directly attached to...the idea of being robbed of one's eyes.*

Turning a blind eye to one's unsightly desires, our scary truths.

The Other Mother in *Coraline* steals her victims' eyes and sews buttons over their vacant sockets.

Thinking of her now, pounding her spider hands on the little door, shrieking, *Don't leave me! Don't leave me!*

When I lived on the train tracks, I kept an anonymous suicide note above my desk: *All this buttoning and unbuttoning.* I wasn't suicidal, just existential.

A cake of soap,
A wedding ring,
A gold filling.
(Plath again)

Speaking of *Coraline*, all this buttoning and unbuttoning could refer to the bouncing between the mundane and the uncanny.

The oscillation between the boring and monstrous.

Thinking about Neil Gaiman...

When he was young, Jim Henson made *Time Piece,* an experimental short on death. (Nominated for an Oscar, it was.) Surreal and rhythmic, set to jazz, the film starts with him in bed—it's uncanny how young he looks. We listen to his heart beat. When his eyes blink they sound like a camera's shutter. This character is alive and watching, recording. From there he's thrown into work clothes. Time moves forward at a terrifying pace, steady on the jazz beat, progressing symbolically as a life should, all sound effects, no dialogue.

Sporadically, handsome young Henson coughs or says, *Help.*

When he paints an elephant pink, I assume that is his death. The uncanny elephant in the room, what we're forever pretending isn't a thing. Annihilation. Nothingness. *That can't be right.* The music reaches a fever pitch. When he's shot out of the sky, six jokes converge into an absurd finale.

His images cluster, play with into one another just as Robin's impressions do, in a kind of moving collage. They're both so cheeky, so quick, toying with our minuscule attention spans, showing more than words alone could.

They both cram more time into minutes.

Does anyone remember *Toys?*

Art comes from a gesture of power turned against itself, Kathy Acker once said. Through plagiarism and pornographic collage, Acker displays the dismembered corpse rearranged according to a desire unfettered by social norms.

Sounds carnivalesque.

Fight the terror of death by making art, making a simulacrum of your own death, so you can control it. So you can understand it. So you can avoid it.

You will still die, safe in your suburban house, she later said in that same interview.

As his grandfather lay dying, Jim cut up his mother's coat and made his first Kermit.

Kermit was born from grief.

The Muppet Show came about just after his brother died.

Grief qua fuel.

The opposite of death is art.

Henson made order out of darkness, such a Kermit thing to do.

A girl's disgust with frogs is a girl's disgust with boys. Blunt male desire can be scary, but represented as an abject slimy little thing triggers the girl's curiosity. Because like a golden egg in the bottom of a well, the girl deep down knows that her fear of frogs is benign and worthy of inspection. As such, the frog is the introduction to the reptilian boy brain.

Hence the Frog Prince archetype.

Robin once played the Frog Prince on Shelley Duvall's *Faerie Tale Theatre*. He was apparently very hungover when he did so, completely wrung out from cocaine and grief as *Mork & Mindy* had just been cancelled. In between takes he would remove the giant papier-mâché frog head and rant to the live audience about television and values. He was insane in that moment, someone said. Sick, I would imagine. Stewing in a frog's head of bad choices. John Belushi had just died of an overdose, too. They had been close. So close they had been together the night he died.

Must have been a special kind of nightmare being so hungover and so sad, wearing the large papier-mâché frog head in all that oppressive green body paint under the hellish spotlights in front of a crowd of actual people. Everyone disappointed in you, too, because they wanted funny, they wanted a taste of legend. They wanted Mork. Not you and your feelings, your addictions and truth.

It's not easy being green.

I think I would've fainted. Or thrown up. Or not gone at all.

Maybe he didn't want to disappoint his Olive Oyl.

For Sartre, emotions are sudden intruders, they offer us only a spontaneous grasp of a situation. He says that when we encounter something so horrible, in our attempt to view it differently, we magically transform the extreme danger by fainting, so that the horrible thing is no longer in our consciousness. We flee from it, as it were.

Vladimir: *Well? Shall we go?*

Estragon: *Yes, let's go.*

They do not move.

Jim Henson wrote his own version of *The Frog Prince*. The girl's tongue is tied in a curse, she can only say her words backwards. Only the frog understands her.

What a metaphor.

At some point, only love will make sense.

Blue skies! was *Sesame Street*'s code phrase for a child on set. Jim would put out his cigarette, put out the existential grimace, and perform like a man who said he was only borrowing the planet from children.

Prince Naveen seems to be devoid of any darkness, the opposite of Hamlet. Cut off financially, he's still a child. He plays music like he plays women. He's a no-account, philandering, lazy bump on a log. So sexy, so frustrating.

Tiana is no fun, she rejects the frog.

Like Belle, Tiana's animus is her lover. Tiana has to learn to embrace the dandy frog slut inside her before she can grow up.

Tiana's a workaholic. How will she feel after she opens that restaurant? Exhausted? Empty? Right at the start of the Great Depression, too. Of course it won't fulfill her. It's not enough. She needs family, friends, laughter, music, life. Duh.

You know you're in a mood when that message is rote.

Unless that message is served to you without art. The kind of movies made by committee, written by AI.

Like a Warhol painting: flat and soulless, a copy of a form.

Like an ad, like the internet, like Kohl's at 1pm.

My biological grandfather called our house one day.

Like it was normal.

I imagine my mom taking the phone from the wall in the kitchen. His voice opening that portal to pathology. I imagine her sitting down at a kitchen table that is probably full of things.

Maybe she disappeared, went somewhere else in that instant. The sound vibrations of her trauma rendering her speechless.

A wound inside is not like a wound outside.

I didn't understand why Cinderella didn't just leave.

Trauma is why Cinderella didn't just leave.

I do not know trauma like this.

To know pain is to know the annihilation of all things.

When you're in agony, little else matters.

Elaine Scarry writes: *To have great pain is to have certainty; to hear that another person has pain is to have doubt.*

Thinking of how much I needed Kate Zambreno's *Heroines*.

She asks: Who gets to become the artist, and who gets locked up?

You desire to write?? How hysterical! Quick, take Virginia's pen away, tell her to lie down.

Cathy Caruth writes, *Trauma seems to be much more than a pathology, or the simple illness of a wounded psyche: it is always the story of a wound that cries out, that addresses us in the attempt to tell us of a reality or truth that is not otherwise available. This truth, in its delayed appearance and its belated address, cannot be linked only to what is known, but also to what remains unknown in our very actions and our language.*

In other words, there is always an absence inside trauma.

Linking it with desire.

Something repressed.

An uncanny stranger.

This void, this spectral of death stays. It caught you once, but then lost its grip and released you. But there are traces of its phantom boney fingers.

Funny how we associate pain with death when it really means that we are very much alive.

But also, we all carry the trauma of our shared history.

Virginia Woolf, Zelda Fitzgerald, Sylvia Plath, their trauma is ours too.

Every woman who dies in childbirth, who's slaughtered by domestic violence, who's been raped to death in war.

We are only as free as the woman next to us.

For Cinderella, the attic is her freedom, a place where she can dream. Until that damned clock chimes, of course, the *old killjoy*.

To dream, in other words, *to create, write*.

Cinderella at least has a room of her own.

That old killjoy ends everything.

The penultimate shot of *Timepiece* is a grandfather clock in the mud.

Just before entering Neverland, the Darlings fly onto Big Ben, then leave reality with its joy killing time behind.

When her stepmother locks her in the attic, it's the mice—her collective animus and tiny army—who free her from her girlhood prison. She tells them they're pretty, worthy, kind. They mirror her. Vermin to vermin: *You matter.*

So this story is in fact the story of how and why Cinderella left. I was wrong, dear reader.

A dream is a wish your heart makes. How terrifying. How Freudian.

If I'm supposed to follow my heart, does that mean every chamber?

My daughter loves No Face, the monster from *Spirited Away*. He stalks the bathhouse and is ignored by everyone. He eats too much, is so lonely. It's not his fault that he ate three people. He reflects human emotions and got caught in a cycle of gluttony and greed. The girl sees this and befriends him, saves him.

Woman's job is to love the unloveable.

Belle trusts the Beast, even though she is afraid he wants to eat her. She wants impossible fulfillment: to adventure in the great wide somewhere. She wants to be an animal, to eat and kill. To think only of herself. But she also wants to fall in love and be devoured. To die again and again.

La petite mort, an emo orgasm.

Sign my death with your teeth, Cixous writes.

Speaking of cake, Belle and Adam (the Beast)—if we're being historically accurate—would've been threatened by the guillotine.

The servants-turned-objects' testimony certainly wouldn't have helped their case.

Rufus could never kill anything, could never be an alpha, he never even tried. When he met Joy Division, my husband's cat, he did his fainting trick and exposed his neck. *Uncle! Uncle!*

During the Roman Empire, for unknown reasons, when kids were attacked by bullies, they wouldn't be set free until they uttered the phrase *Patrue, mi Patruissimo!* Or, *Uncle, my best of uncles!*

This is an internet fact, so do with it what you will.

When we watch *FernGully*, my daughter and me, we talk about how replacing the forest with industry is bad. When my daughter sees people in movies enjoying nature on blankets with lots of fruit, she asks why we thought adding phones was better.

Then she grabs my phone to look at something.

Our shared collective trauma of deforestation.

Rosemary for the forests.

Thoughts and prayers for the forests.

Kathy Acker writes: ***Parents stink***

Never having known a mother, her mother had died when Janey was a year old, Janey depended on her father for everything and regarded her father as boyfriend, brother, sister, money, amusement, and father.

Once upon a time my hometown fell in love with the town next to it, so they copied it like a tween trying on a character, built box after box, now the lots are all empty. *The End.*

So much concrete.

All these vacant storefronts could be trees.

We replicate the wrong things.

The painter David Salle on Kathy Acker: *Her work is seemingly to omnivorously take from anywhere, heedless of where it came from or what it is. There was some inner voice which says this needs this other element and then the two of them seem to require this third and then the three of those require a fourth and it's a bit like improvisational ensemble acting, where the first image is in a sense the premise but what comes out of it—where the characters take it—is completely unpredictable.*

This also reminds me of Williams, of course.

Anxious people tend to watch the same things over and over, the way children do, it soothes them. To know what happens. Because the characters feel like family. Because they're working something out.

Jim Henson's daughter wrote a vignette about capturing endangered frogs in the hopes they'll mate. In it, a rebel bird flies into the rainforest as a refugee from the human world to tell everyone the horror of human appetites. The exotic animals all imagine themselves wrapped in plastic on the black rubber conveyor belt for the faceless, colorless, life-sized people puppets' consumption.

Anxious people also tend to hoard food.

The cognitive dissonance so many of us employ as meat eaters.

Acker died in Room 101, breast cancer ate her alive.

Room 101, of course, refers to *1984*. She had noted this.

Anaïs Nin writes, *People do not live in the present always, at one with it. They live at all kinds of and manners of distance from it, as difficult to measure as the course of planets. Fears and traumas make their journeys slanted, peripheral, uneven, evasive.*

Nin, whose father abandoned her at ten, and then returned twenty years later. To pursue her.

Freud says that life is an awakening out of a death for which there was no preparation. He says that life itself is traumatic, precisely because it comes from un-being, it comes from stasis.

And, since all trauma arises where history is misunderstood, history arises through misunderstanding.

Art, for Freud—specifically literature—exposes the depth of the sense of the uncanny more vividly than the disclosure of the uncanny in real life.

The *je ne sais quoi* of art is that it seems realer than real.

The child intuitively comprehends that although these stories are unreal, *they are not* untrue, writes Bruno Bettelheim.

Lacan focuses on the suddenness of anxiety, especially when the strange and unhomely thing becomes homely.

Some thoughts take a lifetime to unravel.

Lila's *dissolving margins* from *The Neapolitan Novels* suffocate her. The narrator tells us her friend is sometimes afraid that she's a liquid, barely contained. As though she's afraid of the cosmic soup she knows we all are.

She's not wrong though.

When my daughter has a panic attack she says, *I don't feel real.*

This doesn't feel real. Nothing feels real.

Anxiety is like a flood. Inside a panic attack you're caught in a storm, it can feel like you're drowning inside yourself.

Thinking of how many ancient cultures describe a great flood.

Thinking of Theweleit, how men think of women as contained floods.

I smoked to calm my anxiety, I see that now. I didn't see that then, only cigarette after magic cigarette.

It's hard for me to remember that anxiety is an emotion and not a physical condition, a symptom of the sudden end of things.

It may not be that, but it is a premonition. A tremor in the illusion.

How many women were burned for worrying? For being hypochondriacs?

For knowing how plants work?

For grieving?

For their emotional devotion to the old ways?

Is it a waste to give my three wishes to alleviating my physical maladies?

Is this because, essentially, Catholicism told me that my body is not my self? Not *me*.

Kristeva: *[In death it] is no longer I who expel, "I" is expelled. The border has become an object.*

Immediately after Robin Williams died, people began circulating pictures of Genie saying, *Genie, you're free now*. The meme had corroded the message, the present had swallowed the past.

I definitely cried the first time I saw it though.

It does not take much to make me cry.

Sometimes I think I'm addicted to crying.

When I'm not sad, I can rely on narrative catharsis to release.

(I can always rely on *Steven Universe*.)

Release what?

The chaos, I tell my therapist.

The ghosts, the demons.

The grief, *the love*.

Jasmine really didn't know that there were people in her country who didn't have enough to eat, that there was such a thing as money, or an economy, or injustice.

Jasmine, who is *not a prize to be won*, who totally actually is a prize to be bartered.

She is a caged tiger, pacing in her cell. Frustrated, stamping, ready.

But hopeful, we're to surmise. Raja (her animus's name) in Arabic means *hope*.

David Letterman once leaned in to Robin during an interview and asked if he, too, had felt emotional after heart surgery. *Yes!* Robin released and nearly began to cry. These comedy titans had their armor cracked and were dealing with their mortality in between commercial breaks. *And we're back*, Letterman said next. Enough of that.

My daughter calls *Hook, Sad Peter Pan,* because she always cries when lost children are reunited with their parents, which *Hook* both does and doesn't deliver. Because in the beginning, there is also a scene on Peter's origins, how he orphans himself, crawling off into Neverland out of existential spite.

Robin orphans himself again in *Jumanji* too.

In both cases it's because the Robins are afraid, unwilling to grow up.

The remake of *Jumanji* introduced the concept of "lives" to my daughter. The protagonists play a video game, each character gets three lives. She was very jealous of them, then sad.

I got it again, my daughter will frown. *You only get one life.*

If there is a heaven, Vicodin and cigarettes better be there.

And cats. And weed. And books. All of my addictions, please.

Like wouldn't Heaven be *mid* if you couldn't cry?

But any pleasure seems like Hell's domain.

Deconstructing Harry's Hell looks like a good time.

Whereas Dante's Heaven? Meh.

How awesome could light be if it didn't mimic some kind of drug-like euphoria?

God as addiction.

Billy Crystal was a sexy choice for the Devil.

Daddy's out of focus, Robin's kids taunt in a different scene. And they're right, you can't see him, he's blurry, pixilated. An artist, an actor that no one can see clearly, not even his family. *You're soft, Mel. Is it something you ate?* his wife asks.

His wife, played by Julie Kavner (voice of Marge Simpson), offers a symbolic harmony. Her voice a metaphor for motherhood itself.

Julie Kavner, who also plays his love interest in *Awakenings*. She is the only one who believes him. Together, they bring dozens of people back to life.

Sometimes I help my mother organize her house. We move piles of things from one room to the other. Like Sisyphus moving boulders. Rooms and hallways all lined with furniture, knick-knacks, glassware, holiday decorations, folksy art, projects. *Pretty things*, she calls them. Collections. Lots of things that were to become other things in these piles too. Crafts in potentia.

Again, Nin: *Again and again I have entered realism, and found it arid, limited.*

Girl, same.

Stories are better, prettier, they feel less empty to me.

Pretty things.

Give me the fires of conflict and the waters of resolution.

Paradoxes and passion or bust.

At the apartment with the bed that birthed and swallowed the train, I had a large standing mirror that reminded me of Sabina's mirror from *The Unbearable Lightness of Being*. I painted it blood red and hung a bowler hat from one of its curlicue shoulders. On its surface my brilliant friend wrote, *You are Anaïs's heir apparent.*

This feels embarrassing to tell you.

Nonetheless, I persisted.

Sincere, bite-sized, politicized feminism chafes me, like forcing STEM down all our throats.

Let it be said, neither Robin Williams nor Jim Henson have been posthumously #metoo-ed; and both, it is said, had a thing for the ladies. Neither, also, has appeared on any Epstein list.

Now, the men in my mother's family are all genial, agreeable, forgettable. They are not the main characters.

Now, her family is a matriarchy. They won't make that mistake again.

They trade crowns in this matriarchy. Spokes on a wheel that's been broken.

Like Saint Catherine's body, tied to a wheel and broken on the altar of male ego.

In kindergarten, I began school at Saint Catherine's. They had a stained-glass window of her with a wheel, facing a cut and carved Jesus on a the cross.

When I feel crazy, I stretch and rake the carpet with my fingernails. I make pretty onion shapes around my body and I cry.

This is me, working through the ogres in my blood.

Ogres have layers, you know, like an onion.

There is this meme of Lisa Simpson all wild-eyed and rocking I like to send my husband when I'm like this.

He calls this my Gena Rowlands routine.

Francey Russell asks, *Who can watch Gena Rowlands's character have a nervous breakdown in John Cassavetes's* A Woman Under the Influence *(1974) and not think,* A human body is not meant to move like that. *The film is painful to watch not (just) because we see a character in unspeakable pain, but because we see a real human being going through the undeniable physical contortions of pain. You can reassure yourself that it's "just a movie" or it's "just acting." But that body is real, and something real is happening to it.*

The Gena in me comes when I need to create, almost invariably this will happen after I ovulate, when I'm steeped in the sad half of my moons.

When I long to gush.

This has become more pronounced after thirty-five, but I only recently learned that perimenopause is a thing.

There's so much we weren't taught.

Anne Carson said Emily Brontë used to claw the carpet too. She was the crazy sister, the cruel one.

Wuthering Heights is cruel.

I like happy endings. I'm a more of a Jane than a Catherine.

I used to think I was a Catherine, but I just wanted a Heathcliff.

Heathcliff as lover in absence, as a symbol for longing. I liked that.

Transforming a lover into a symbol puts you in the place between the lover and the symbol, that's the place of desire. My best friend said that, or maybe she said Anne Carson said that.

With Heathcliff, as with any illicit lover, what's so enticing is the threat and beauty of pain. The pain of vulnerability, of a desire so potent it blossoms into a problem.

Milan Kundera: *Physical love is unthinkable without violence.*

Then there is Jane Eyre, sensible Jane, the OG archetype for the angry teen girl.

But like Beyoncé, she stays, she forgives. But only once he's humbled.

Only once he loses his eyes.

Furious, Jane is openly critical of marriage and religion. She sees the patriarchy everywhere. She looks at all of it then screams, *Death first!* and runs like a wild woman to live, sleep, starve on the moors.

Jane to Rochester: *I am no bird; and no net ensnares me; I am a free human being with an independent will, which I now exert to leave you.*

The moors that are not only full of wind and wolves, but werewolves, vampires, and black hellhounds. These are the creatures that eat women, these are the metaphors of marriage and sex. The lunacy of wanting to be caged and devoured.

Just before Jane had said that, Rochester says: *Jane, be still; don't struggle so like a wild, frantic bird, that is rending its own plumage in its desperation.*

Jane, don't be hysterical, it isn't becoming. Don't make me put you in the attic.

Ha ha ha, Grace Poole laughs.

Jane requires marriage on equal terms. She is not insane. (Neither was Bertha.)

Emily, however, lets Catherine go languorously psychotic.

Catherine watches the moonlit moors, watches their tumult, feels their swells as she watches her old house from her new house. Her Heathcliffhouse from her Lintonhouse. Her then from her now. Her heart from her head.

Looking at the nouns in Catherine's lovers' names: heat and cliff versus lint. What's more boring than lint? Fire and falling will kill you.

Heathcliff, once the goblin in the basement, now owns Wuthering Heights.

His and her madness took over the house, is the house. When Catherine dies of brain fever, her ghost haunts that house.

Rochester has to literally go blind in order to see a woman as an equal, not a doll he could keep, a pretty bird he could cage.

How uncanny.

You open your eyes like an eager bird. Rochester loves this about her. But then this bird thinks? How peculiar, how confusing, how, perhaps, off-putting.

How uncanny.

Both Brontë heroines already knew the power—the exquisite torture—of watching.

To watch someone is to connect with them, to bring them in.

This act can feel wildly intimate.

This is why people can't control themselves around celebrities, they think they know them.

This projected intimacy wins elections.

Robin suffered from Lewy Body Dementia. He never knew he had LBD, but he knew something was wrong, that he wasn't *himself.*

His widow made a movie about it, *Robin's Wish*. She's become one of the disease's leading spokepeople. *The terrorist inside my husband's brain*, she called LBD. Once the disease enters its final stages, the victim isn't able to make their own decisions, the disease takes over their lucidity, their ego dissolves. Like savage spores do to those ants.

Like Lila's dissolving margins.

Like his worst nightmare.

He would be locked in an attic, in other words.

He wanted to relinquish his own "I," a last act of control.

His bits were always so controlled. Crazed, wild, everyone said, but no, controlled.

When I first heard about his death, I felt sad that I wouldn't be able to know him.

I wouldn't have asked him to entertain me. He could've been real.

Whatever that means.

Sometimes, when you watch him, you can see a surly layer underneath all the movement, under all that unfettered happy.

I would've liked to have made him happy, even if just for a moment. To be with him when he wasn't on.

As Rainbow Randolph, he was a deranged derivation of himself, manic and on but corrupt, vain, and exiled. Wild, desperately unhappy, unhinged and dark, but not creepy, not flat *One Hour Photo* Robin. Bipolar Robin.

Like that episode of *My Little Pony* when happy happy Pinkie Pie thinks her friends don't like her.

A long enough time ago, my cliché New York Freudian analyst told me that I wasn't responsible for my mother's happiness. This analyst didn't find me very interesting. For him it was rote, but for me I hadn't yet realized that healing generational trauma meant healing myself.

Encanto misses this message too.

I was disappointed because I knew that somewhere inside it was both true and not true that I wanted an Anaïs/Otto Rank relationship.

Otto Rank, who wrote *The Trauma of Being Born.*

Anaïs, who searched and searched for father-lovers to fill the father-sized hole, thought letting the real deal into her bed would cure. Madness, everyone said, but no, controlled.

Laughter and tears are not separate experiences, with intervals of rest: they rush out together and it is like walking with a sword between your legs, she wrote from within her *House of Incest.*

I wanted my analyst, at least, to want me. But first, he would've had to have been interested in me. Maybe if I told him that he would've been.

But I doubt it.

And that's not at all what I wanted.

I also never got to sleep with any of my teachers.

I had heard one of my college professors had a thing for his students, but he wasn't my type: frail, soft-spoken, into poetry, encouraging without discernment. He was nice.

I think my high school science teacher would've been the only one where it was possible. He was young, I was fifteen. I met him in his shitty classroom office once and he cried about how hard it was to be a teacher, how the kids never listened to him. His classroom was usually unruly. This teacher would write me hall passes to find my friends in the lunchroom or meet a lover on the stairwell. He'd let them attend class with me too. I was a good student, it was fine. Such an idyllic setting: the smell of shop class next door, the gray metal shelving, the open cardboard boxes teeming with glassware gone white with age, dust motes in sunlight, privacy. As this baby teacher cried and confessed, I comforted him, I held his arm and something inside me stirred. But I couldn't do that to him. I couldn't throw my hormonal, nubile body onto his. This guy needed love.

When Shakespeare was fifteen, a woman named Katherine Hamlet fell into the Avon and drowned.

"Fell."

I would describe fifteen as the year I went mad.

My migraines were beginning to settle then, too.

Robin's Popeye was one of my first real crushes. He had needs, that man.

When I was eight-ish I couldn't stop throwing up blood. In the hospital the TV reran *Popeye* over and over and over. It was an awakening, a comfort, my own personal Patch Adams.

Later, reading Oliver Sacks's book on migraines, I learned that children who throw up excessively can predict severe migraines later in life.

I used to throw up in my sleep all the time.

It was just anxiety but.

(Your body is not safe.)

This memory of the unnecessary hospital visit, haunting me still, like *Popeye'*s set. Built and forgotten, rotting and useless. Invasive. The place is real, but it's a set. A set is real as a set, not a village, and yet, it can be visited. In Italy! This dilapidated set, making it both real and fabricated.

Uncanny houses.

Olive Oyl lives with her parents in their home that they've converted to an inn. They are the only place that will take in the strange sailor; they've also taken in a Jew and a thief. As her mother is busy, it becomes Olive's job to show Popeye to his room. She tells him that his name is *pretty strange. Popeye...*, she muses, referring to his "squinky eye." Unfamiliar. The whole one-eye thing, of course, is a euphemism for a dick. She takes him past her room and shames him for looking in it. Her name, he mutters under his breath, is a kind of lubricant and therefore, pretty strange as well. Alluring.

Olive can't get the key to open the lock. He offers to help, his one-eye cocked and his phallic corncob pipe gripped between his teeth. Very suddenly the door opens which violently throws Olive Oyl to the window. Olive Oyl, who's so thin with her noodle arms, is carried off by a gust of wind. She moans the way she does, hurt but sexy, and grabs the window shades for leverage. They spring open, flap flap flapping like piano scrolls. Embarrassed of her orgasm, she drops her gaze. He proceeds to attempt to put his baggage onto the bed, a bed inside her parents' house, a bridal bed. She tries to prevent him and lands in the bed first, then a lamp falls onto the bed with her, a lightbulb, an idea, the bed breaks, collapses into itself like a neutron star from the sheer weight of her passion for this strange sailor. She moans again, a picture falls, Popeye is very amused and kind of scared.

Later that night, after Olive runs away from her engagement party, Popeye escorts her farther, down toward another path. He's carrying her baggage now, not his own where's my father baggage but her she must marry baggage. Olive must leave her father but is reluctant. When Popeye sets down her luggage, one basket is replaced with another by a mysterious set of hands seemingly unattached from a body. The hands of God, mayhaps. An Ace of Cups. This other basket has a baby inside of it. The couple takes the baby and their encounter earlier is then symbolically understood.

Olive Oyl even looks like Anaïs Nin.

And then there's also that whenever Robin impersonates his penis, which he has done many, many times, he squinks his eye and busts out his Popeye voice.

Robin Williams, who of course, was classically trained. Juilliard. Shakespeare. Etc.

Just before that hospital stay, I used to pass out, too. I carried chocolate around with me like I was Professor Lupin, like at any moment I would need to ward off a dementor attack.

The dementor attack being a panic attack.

Like Harry, I'm afraid of the fear itself.

But I would literally pass out.

Now, I'm just afraid I will.

I like to think that in another life I was a priestess, but I don't believe in other lives. I barely believe in this one.

Though, if we are reincarnated, I'm sure I died of tuberculosis in one of my lives.

Was burned at the stake in another.

Childbirth too, naturally, probably a few times there.

When my aunt dropped to her knees and screamed like an animal, it was then I knew that I loved her despite whether or not she loved me. I assume she does, as her sister's daughter, maybe. She would if she had held my raw grief, instead of I hers. We don't see each other much, not irl or on social media, only in the background of my mom's happy facetime calls. I am used to her as an on and off fixture for my mother.

When they fight, they separate for years. It's often over politics, but really it's what they won't talk about.

My mom doesn't feel whole when her sister's cold.

I am so afraid of the migraines that will be inside my grief.

I can never completely indulge in crying without one.

Somedays I cry all day though, the tears quietly streaming down my face like two blue rivers. Those are the days that turn into dark nights with my favorite ice pack. It was a birthday present, we call it, *the birthday icepack*. I am very attached to it.

I like characters who cry too: Moaning Murtle, Blue Diamond, Luisa, Sadness.

I like that episode in *The Sopranos* when Carmela just cries and fights and cries.

That's allergies, my neurologist said. *The crying.*

I thought it was hereditary, part of my lore. Inherited grief.

But really, I have severe allergies to ragweed, the pretty yellow wildflowers that line the road.

I think it's still related, still symbolic when one's immune system goes haywire over nothing. When one's body convinces itself the mundane is demonic and must be destroyed.

I know this pathology's villain origin story.

All the women in my mother's family have autoimmune disorders.

I'm waiting for my diagnosis. Though migraines seem as though they are part of the femme constellation of autoimmune diseases. The we don't know why you have chronic pain cluster.

It took me my whole life to figure out I was allergic to makeup. Because it doesn't give me a headache every time, just sometimes. But sometimes means it's possible every time. Not that that matters, because now it's nearly every time anyway. That's how my banana allergy took hold, too. I could eat them sometimes, they always tasted like needles, but now my throat swells.

Bananas cross-react with ragweed. I'm not actually allergic to bananas, but I still can't eat them.

Oh, the metaphors inside a banana allergy.

Puking, for me, begets puking, and sometimes I wasn't able to stop until my throat would split and petals of blood would fall into the toilet water. In the hospital, no one would tell me what was wrong. On the slab I thrashed as they poked and swabbed. On the third day

I told them I was feeling much better. When the nurse left, my mother furrowed her brow and told me not to tell them that.

So inside this trauma I fell in love with Popeye's bulging forearms, the way he looked at Olive, that mutter. I lay with Robin in that boring hospital bed where I felt fine but the adults told me I was sick.

I left a part of myself in that traumatic hospital bed, shed a skin, as it were, and felt myself grow up, just a little bit, just enough.

In the end, they had no idea what was wrong with me.

(Because it was just serious anxiety.)

I know it's time to let Rufus go, but he's still in there. His eyes are not vacant. He still wants things, still yells at me for things.

How can you just decide it's time to kill your friend?

I sang Olive Oyl's song to my barbies like a private siren song, excited to someday be old enough to love a boy like that. But more excited still for a boy to love me like that.

Maybe it's because he's so alone.
Maybe it's because he never had a home.
He needs me. He needs me. He needs me. He needs me. He needs me. He needs me.

Rufus chirrups when I sing him this song. He likes quiet songs, he's afraid of the tanks rolling through my husband's symphonies.

It's interesting how owning stuff now flipped classes.

It's embarrassing to own things now.

I don't think I own Rufus. That's not right. But he is my responsibility.

Carrying donkeys is not Luisa's responsibility, it's the donkey herder's, who clearly does not have as much to do as Luisa does.

Thinking of Mirabel, whom the *Encanto* didn't think deserved a room of her own.

If Mirabel's gift is to heal the family's trauma—and by heal, I mean reveal and hold—then that *is* a kind of superpower. But the *Encanto* then is asking her to set aside her life, her ego, and serve. Though all of the women in the *Encanto* serve the *Encanto*, they all get magic. They each get their own special room, except for Mirabel, who we're told has no magical gift.

One can argue, though, that Pepa's gift doesn't really serve anyone (save for the audience's comedic relief). She's the hysteric of the family, the designated "sick" one, even dressed in yellow wallpaper. If she were to become grief-stricken, the town would be in ruins.

I consider my things horcruxes. Witnesses, at least. Art objects, witch totems, tangible memories with pieces of my soul stuffed inside. Useless to anyone else, or at least, emptier.

We each think the other's tower of meaning is faulty, my parents and me.

Stretch this microcosm and allow it to be a metaphor for the current crisis of meaning.

They don't understand why I don't just pray anyway. Like an insurance policy.

I look to art.

I believe in art the way other people believe in God, Lidia Yuknavitch says.

#metoo

But like all divinity, it constantly needs to be renewed.

My mom said a prayer with my daughter the other day. I didn't love it.

My mother's the eldest but she has the most fun when pretending to be six. She really likes being a grandmother to littles.

My mom has come home before to find everything she thought she owned on the curb. Well, all that was left.

In my littlekid middle class toy palace, she would tell me stories of loving one thing—a bike, a ring—only to have it taken, left on a soap dish, gone. I would feel so bad late at night for littlekid mom.

These days I'm taking lots of long winter walks while Stephen Fry reads me *Sherlock Holmes*.

I will miss this when it is over.

There must be a word for deeply missing something before you've lost it? When you suddenly see the present as past and it breaks you.

Tocka: a longing with nothing to long for?

Litost: torment at the sudden sight of one's own misery?

That meme of the guy gesturing to a butterfly: *Is this love?*

I try to pay every scrap of attention to my daughter, but that's not always possible. Sometimes mommy's having a panic attack. Sometimes she's Gena Rowlands.

Sometimes her margins are dissolving.

Mommy's out of focus.

Sometimes she's with a client, helping other people finish their books. Sometimes she's on an important phone call with a doctor. Sometimes there's no head space for all the questions. Sometimes her head hurts as much as when she birthed the near ten pounds of you.

> *Does every animal get its own hell?*
> *What do you think elf hell's like?*
> *What happened on the worst day of your life?*

I'm on the Goddamn call of my life, Sad Peter Pan yells at his children.

It's the record scratch moment. He yells at his kids for having fun, the jerk.

Who the fuck wouldn't yell at their kids in that moment on that phone call?

> *Have you ever fallen in love before Daddy?*
> *Would you rather never stand up or never sit down?*
> *Who does my mushy cereal look like?*

The answer, dear reader, was Alvin, Simon, and Theodore. I had guessed correctly.

I've gone mad trying to decipher the difference between a virus and an infection. Between physical illness and mental illness.

I've found exhaustion corrodes depression, but this kind of exhaustion is only possible with responsibility.

So really, responsibility corrodes depression.

When Robin Williams finished one of his cocaine-driven standup shows, he was beyond exhausted, depleted, they said. Mentally, physically, and emotionally drained. He left it all on the stage, they said.

What did he watch to relax? What did he eat?

Famously, Einstein maybe said, *If you want your children to be intelligent, read them fairy tales. If you want them to be very intelligent, read them more fairy tales.*

The present corrodes the past, just as all memes corrode the present. We are bombarded with them daily, they flood our brain space. They exhaust without ever exhausting, and they're quick, like drugs. So we're addicted.

Einstein did answer a letter once, to a Miss Block. She asked about the point of living amidst all this war. *Dear Miss Block*, he writes, *The question "Why" in the human sphere is easy to answer: to create satisfaction for ourselves and for other people. In the extra-human sphere the question has no meaning. Also the belief in God is in no way out for in this case you may ask: "Why God".*

When morality is spelled out to children in perfunctory lessons, they roll their eyes, but when they decode the symbols woven through a story, what unravels is insight and epiphany, which builds confidence, not contempt.

Now Rufus *only* wants to eat coconut oil. He's starving. I think this is keeping him alive. He's all jagged bones but his coat is so shiny and soft. The vet didn't know what to do with that.

Margaret Atwood wrote a story about a woman who lives off of creamy, oily spa products.

I think of her a lot, Toby from *The Year of the Flood.*

I think of how Margaret said that she didn't put a thing in *The Handmaid's Tale* that hadn't already happened somewhere before.

While at school, my daughter played a game where she was two other girls' "lowly assistant." She had cleaning duties, straightening pillows of leaves and such. Readying myself to talk about class, she said she liked being the protagonist. Because when you're poor, kind, and suffering, she said, *It's all about you.*

When you're sick or dying, it's all about you.

Except if you're a mom. Moms get sick and die all the time, in the background.

That meme of Loki saying, *Yes, that's very sad. Anyway.*

Moms die at the beginning of the story. Mom death is prologue and necessary for the child to grow up and into an adult. Mom can't be there, making decisions, telling Elsa to maybe calm down and not run away and freeze the summer. Because Elsa has to run away. She has to fail. That's the story.

To hold your child is to know you're going to die, Christopher Hitchens had said.

Not that Elsa's parents were good parents. They're told by the magic troll doctor that fear will destroy her, will be her undoing. So, they isolate her, severely. Tell her to bottle all of her emotions. *Conceal it, don't feel it, don't let it show.* Then they leave her in her freezing room, scared and alone. For years.

They even had special chains forged, ones that would shackle her hands in iron mittens, just in case.

When she runs away, it's clear that she's processing the trauma from isolation, from inept parenting. Creating the storm, her ice palace and dress, the song, this is her art therapy.

Elsa is an art monster.

Elsa has no love interest either, and her "child," Olaf, hangs with Anna, is Anna's animus.

Elsa's art space is more of a hermetic moment of rest (sure, that she temporarily fantasizes is permanent) than a complete shirking of duties. Symbolically, I think, we don't teach our daughters the advantages of solitude because the myths of genius are masculine. She, instead, is told to get back and take care of everyone. Literally as queen.

Though later, in the sequel, she'll gift that responsibility to Anna too.

Elsa needs to put her own oxygen mask on first.

Disney said this is Elsa fighting her inner Ice Queen, because they drifted so far from their source material.

In a world without Anna though, Elsa collapses, so sad, so done, she conjures the ice sword for Hans to use. As the eldest daughter, knowing Anna was neglected too, Elsa feels as though she's now Anna's parent.

Both girls need therapy.

Elsa resonated so virally because she takes the archetype of the sad girl and makes it powerful.

As much as the sister story is sweet, and mega successful, it would've been something for them to have been faithful to Anderson's *Snow Queen*.

Ever tried. Ever failed. No matter. Try again. Fail again. Fail better.

Elsa would've blown an ice shard into Kristoff's eye, a piece of her mirror, turning him mean, turning him into her. Anna would've walked through the seasons to rescue him, scenes so lush and laden with symbolism. The gorgeous slumber of spring. The erotic lure of summer. The dashing dangers of autumn.

Alas.

The internet says Elsa's bipolar. Like an official Disney someone said that.

Without trauma, children can't fathom sexual relationships. Early crushes tend toward animals, aliens, or beasts. Like foxes, chipmunks, and frogs. They're safe because they're impossible, but trouble because they're wild.

This obfuscation is like having a crush on sexuality itself, aroused by the thought of arousal.

Robin Williams loved women. *Loved*, they say. Throbbing python of love loved. Watch him pursue in *Good Morning Vietnam* as though it were destiny. *Carpe diem! Rip those bodices!*

Thinking of Lovelace's *couch of perpetual indulgence* too.

Throbbing python of love being a bit of his. It's full of dick euphemisms.

They say the girls fell into his lap, just as his characters always chase them there.

This love, of course, destroyed his first marriage. She had once said that she could've tolerated his philandering, so long as he came home. But then he left with the nanny. How easy it must be to fall in love with the woman loving on your child. Soon enough he married the nanny and had two more kids. It lasted a while, but they eventually divorced as well.

Divorce is like ripping a man's genitals through his wallet, he had said. In time, the quote has morphed to the much more wholesome: *Divorce is like ripping your heart out through your wallet.* More on brand for the people pimping his ass postmortem.

Pimping his ass, the phrase his agent used to refuse to allow Terry Gilliam to credit his performance in *The Adventures of Baron Munchausen.* Instead, his pseudonym reads Ray D. Tutto, a pun on *King of Everything.*

The King of Everything, who separates his head from his body to regulate time and direct comets. To be free, he says. He despises his body with its vulgar appetites, its flatulence and orgasms.

I'm back! Your elephant of joy! He calls to his wife once his head and his body are reunited.

Freud said Medusa's face was a cunt, decorated as it were, with hundreds of dangling, hissing, throbbing pythons. One look, one glance, and the male gaze freezes, aroused, intoxicated, impuissant, castrated, stoned in time, forever hard. For one capsulated second, the instant it takes to recognize the face of a lover, the ripple of an orgasm, he is happy, staring, laughing, adoring. Then he is dead.

There is a mystifying power in this misogyny.

This power leads to crimes of passion, to witch burnings, bones broken on wheels.

Hélène Cixous writes, *Men say that there are two unrepresentable things: death and the feminine sex. That's because they need femininity to be associated with death: it's the jitters that gives them a hard-on! for themselves! They need to be afraid of us. Look at the trembling Perseuses moving backward toward us, clad in apotropes.*

Miss Piggy is my apotrope.

It's a tragedy, what's become of the Muppets, of Miss Piggy. She used to be a star, desire incarnate. A selfish prima donna, but secure, she once had a tremendous power over Kermit. A true Queen of Wands, temper included. She *lived* to desire and be desired.

Kermit is so jazzed that this beguiling sexpot pig loves him that he's willing to overlook her narcissism.

Pigs are a uterine animal, they represent abundance and the Mother Goddess. They never hoard their food (or their love), they eat it as they find it, including, sometimes, their own. Symbolically, they are part of the life-death-life cycle. Their chthonic tusks point down to the earth and are shaped like crescent moons.

With the rise of the masculine monotheisms, it became forbidden to eat the pig's dirty familiar flesh because of its association with the Goddess and sensuality.

Couldn't you make an exception for little old moi?
Miss Piggy asks the cop.
Not even for little old vous!

Also like the Goddess, Miss Piggy carries her feminine rage deep inside her chest. When threatened, she unleashes a torrent of fury until the men yield.

Make your fairy tale pig male though and you often get Orwell's pigs, evil despot pigs. The greedy, brutish capitalists from *Animal Farm* are the opposite of Kermit. Henson's Kermit runs a two-bit comedy sketch show with a bunch of misfits who never listen. He is not famous, he is not glamorous. With his chipped mug, dilapidated studio, and shoestring budget, he routinely shelves his mounting anxiety and calms the chaos enough to put on a successful show.

Kermit's practical, he's already a dad, but a dad who forgot along the way that he's also a red-blooded frog.

The pig brings it out in him. Kermit's unwillingness to commit complements Miss Piggy's unwillingness to settle. She keeps Kermit waiting at places while she is either with or on the phone with other men. These other men want her in some way, increasing her star power. Perpetually humbled, Kermit feels small as he waits.

Now, Post-Henson/Oz, Piggy is an insecure, lonely professional fashion designer who rises to the top *despite* being a pig. She is an undesirable spinster. She is gross, no longer an icon because she's no longer desirable, she is a collection of fat jokes. People are openly disgusted with her appetites. She's constantly wrestling with how hungry she is, openly eating her feelings—her problems—to the point of revulsion. They made her too much. This sad Piggy is obsessed with Kermit, there are no others. They made her pure, they made her ugly and desperate. Her anger insipid, her fat the star.

Thus rendering Kermit's feelings schizophrenic. He pities her, he loves her, he doesn't want her.

Frank Oz spoke as though the current owners of The Muppets were resurrecting a lifeless corpse: *The soul's not there.*

The Muppets are now uncanny.

They crushed the subtle symbolism and went for stale and obvious.

An allegory for most children's stories today.

Frank Oz also said, *The Disney deal is probably what killed Jim. It made him sick.*

Right after Henson's death the company recreated two Victorian ghost stories: *A Christmas Carol* and *Treasure Island*. As nothing ever stays academic, or alive, the company has since been dragging this dead genius's specter from pop flop to disappointment.

Resurrecting his corpse to reify his brand.

Muppet's Most Wanted is the only modern iteration that's worth a damn, imho. While Piggy's character is still disappointing, the rest is good. Except for Walter. I find Walter pointless.

On my *night desk*—as my daughter calls it—stands a PVC figure of Walter. Earlier we pretended he was our waiter. She likes to tease me with Walter, she likes to hear me say he is useless. She laughs and laughs at how useless Walter is.

Fort/Da is game children play. *Fort* meaning *Gone. Da* meaning *There*. Freud says it's to cope with mom leaving the room, or worse, the house.

Just before high school, we fled the South Side suburbs of Chicago because I was being bullied.

My mom told me to be nice to my bullies, to *kill them with kindness.*

I wanted to burn forgiveness to the ground.

I wanted to run away, disappear into my room and write everything I wasn't saying.

What does *The Incredibles* teach us? Fathers and sons are strong, fast, resilient. Mothers are stretched thin. Daughters disappear, until they learn to shield themselves.

Why are you so angry? My mom asks me.

Why aren't you *angry, Mom??*

Because in comparison my childhood was bliss but.

I was bullied out of Catholic school for my arm hair. That's what they glommed onto, how dark my arm hair was, is. But really, I was "mouthy" and an insufferable know-it-all, an atheist, a bitch.

Guilty! Guilty!

Witches have dark hair, so do mistresses and foreigners. The others.

The sacrificed women that maintain the purity of the others.

These women were burned alive to spare the crops and children, the unborn. But really, to kill all the midwives and make way for the white coats.

To burn all the pagan knowledge of the land.

Dodie Bellamy: *A hanged witch's face swells, distorting her ears and lips. Her eyelids turn blue, her eyes turn red and project forwards, sometimes forced out of their cavities. A bloody froth sometimes escapes from her lips and nostrils; sometimes her tongue protrudes. Her fingers clench. It is not uncommon for a hanged witch to expel urine and feces at the moment of her death.*

These women died green and lumpy, pocked with scabs and scars. Their haggard faces with blood-matted hair gave them that cartoon Halloween witch look.

My only nightmares as a child were about standing trial against some god on a very high chair.

Sometimes it was God, sometimes the Devil.

Not the sap trapped in his own ice. More like the Tarot's Devil, claws perched on his cement throne.

Virginia Woolf: *Women who did not apologize for their literary efforts were defined as mad and monstrous: freakish because "unsexed" or freakish because sexually "fallen."*

Freud asks: What if our childself was right along?

What if children have the world better figured out than the adults?

Freud: *The uncanny is that class of the terrifying that leads back to something long known to us, once very familiar.*

A vagina, he'll muse.

We learn to disassociate in the womb, victims of generational trauma.

So Virginia Woolf goes to the shelf and grabs Professor Trevelyan's *History of England*. She writes, *Once more I looked up Women, found "the position of," and turned to the pages indicated. "Wife-beating," I read, "was a recognised right of man, and was practiced without shame by high as well as low...Similarly," the historian goes on, "the daughter who refused to marry the gentleman of her parents' choice was liable to be locked up, beaten and flung about the room, without any shock being inflicted on public opinion.*

There was a study on epigenetics and pregnant women who survived 9/11 and now had PTSD. The study suggests that these women passed down their PTSD to their babies. Because the babies later had the same lowered cortisol, the same heightened stress responses. Two genes, FKBP5 and STAT5B, inhibit glucocorticoid receptors. Heightened glucocorticoid receptor activity is noted in people with PTSD. Variations in FKBP5 are associated with the severity of PTSD symptoms in individuals who suffered child abuse.

In other words, trauma leaves epigenetic marks.

Flung about the room.

Traces. Echoes. Ghosts. Demons.

What Dreams May Come Robin says: *You don't have to break in half to love somebody.*

A film whose depiction of the afterlife is legit horrifying.

My mother's pain echoes in me. Just as her mother's echoed in her, and her mother's echoed in her. A nesting doll of women locked inside father fists, caged inside their pathetic rage.

He that breaks a thing to find out what it is has left the path of wisdom, Gandalf, meaning Tolkien, says.

My mother broke the cycle and married kindness.

You don't have to be a feminist all the time, she once said.

A therapist also once told me *that stuff* didn't matter in a relationship.

What?

I never wanted to be uptight when I grew up. I never wanted to be the mom from *Mrs. Doubtfire.*

And yet, her husband left her to do everything on her own. She had no choice but to become the boring bitch. She despises this about herself, but resents him even more. It didn't have to be this way. Daniel's perpetual joy transformed her into something she didn't like. She had to leave him, to rediscover herself, to get out of a different sort of cage. She had to leave him because she deserves better. She had to leave him so that he could save himself.

But how could she not recognize her lover's eyes? Her instincts must be dead. How could she not know? If I were leaving my kids in the care of a total stranger I would study their eyes, look into their soul. Surely, something would've felt *off* about Euphegenia Doubtfire. You'd smell the uncanny.

You'd see the familiar inside the unfamiliar.

Daniel needed to grow up but felt he couldn't do so without regressing, without Norman Bates-ing himself into his mother.

Still in love with Miranda, Daniel tries to manipulate her by mothering her too, using the old paternalistic codex to slut shame her back into his bed.

Fail better, Daniel.

Though, it is interesting that he pantomimes mothering to learn how to father.

Because he's also replacing Miranda as mother, he then rivals her instincts with his mother's conservatism.

Where does that leave the self inside the character Daniel Hillard? Somewhere oscillating from child to grandmother. He is just skating from one extreme to the other, and we're to suppose he ends up learning a lesson, but to me, the lesson seems lost.

Also, when he finally does show up to parent, he does so with different values. Is this Daniel finally admitting his mother was right? If so, then why didn't he want to talk to her on the phone? Why is he still avoiding her?

Did Miranda know his mom? She must've. I never read the book.

I do appreciate that they ended still divorced.

However, I was very happy that Beyoncé's *Lemonade* ended with them back together.

Robin cannot be in a film without the audience's awareness that he is Robin Williams.

As is, Robin lives twice, as it were, up there and out there.

But sadly no longer out there.

I miss him. We all do. But the him he wrote, the him we've seen ourselves inside of.

Film viewers are always shuttling between realities, between the fictional world and the real world...All film viewing involves this toggling back and forth. The weird joy of it is constitutive of the pleasure of film. The real insists within the fiction, writes Francey Russell.

Thinking of how impossible it is to watch *The Cosby Show* now.

Now thinking of Johnny Depp stopping Amber Heard's pen.

F. Scott Fitzgerald stealing his wife's words then sending her to an asylum, where she had been strapped to her bed and burned alive.

The bodies live-action *Mulan* steps on. Is this serious? Is this a circus?

Thinking of Robin in *Good Morning Vietnam*, of the war on funny he fought, the right to make people happy. Thinking of Forest Whitaker's character saying to him, *So, if I were you, I'd think about suicide.*

Harvey Weinstein also raped Robin out of *Good Will Hunting*'s spoils. Silent Bob writes that there was a *back-end deal* where Robin would've taken home a larger portion of the profits if the film made over one hundred million dollars, which it was definitely about to do. He would've split the money with Weinstein's Miramax, but if our villain released the DVD instead, Miramax would get all the money. Weinstein released the DVD.

As Rufus is diabetic, he gets four clicks of the pen twice a day. The needle goes into the thick scruff of neck. He doesn't care, and will even sleep through it, if I do it. One hundred dollars each, these shots cost, one hundred dollars every four weeks. Until the pharmacist asked me if I was ethically opposed to claiming him as my son.

I would've had him at nineteen. Four years older than my mother's mother.

He was so fat, my teenage son, he couldn't drape his stubby arm over his body. He would lay with my teddy bear, his back against a pillow, sitting up like a human so he could lick his great round belly. Not that he bathed himself often, when he got around to it.

The shots don't seem to be helping anymore though. Skin draped over bones.

The way the dying transform is uncanny.

Like when my dad takes off his glasses, like he took off a piece of his face.

Or like watching Robin in *One Hour Photo*. It's unnerving.

His final days were a *nightmare* his wife had said. He wasn't himself. He was raving and breaking.

He was losing control of it all. He was paranoid, crying all the time, not sleeping, unraveling.

His wife didn't want us all to think something that wasn't true, didn't want us to think it was depression. She didn't want his memory sullied.

Who lives? Who dies? Who tells your story?

Senile, the house has become Rufus's litter box. He can't remember how to get down from places, sometimes he tries to enter the wall, or crawl under furniture with no space for him. He paws and he paws to nowhere.

My widowed aunt is a taxidermist, she could stuff Rufus. I could keep him forever.

Too bad we're only a facsimile of a family.

Not that I would anyway, that would be too creepy.

But it is too bad.

Much like the CGI horror show, *The Lion King*. How dead all the animals look. It really is the epitome of the phenomenon of the uncanny valley.

How long would I see it—as it wouldn't be him but an it—out of the corner of my eye and think, *Hi, Roof!*

Jim Morrison's partner wept on his dead body for days.

I keep all my daughter's milk teeth in a glass vial. When I held her first tooth, I had a strong urge to swallow it. As though this tooth could regrow a girlfish that I could keep safe forever in my belly.

The sea creatures are an extension of Ariel's subconscious. They're her instinct, the waters she can trust. They represent what she's not saying, doubly so as she has no literal voice. So when they sing, *Kiss the Girl*, the fish are speaking for her, *they are her*. Those banning the song for its "rapey intention" are erasing female agency.

Ha ha ha, Grace Poole laughs.

Once upon a time, *The Little Mermaid* used to be seen as a feminist text because more than anything Ariel says, *I want*. The whole narrative centers around her desire.

Her iconic red hair was only so to separate her from the blonde mermaid in *Splash*. Ariel was supposed to be blonde too.

Flounder, her other animus, is a coward but ever-encouraging. Alas, she has outgrown him. He's no help for this fish out water. Men and their dry masculine land masses are treacherous.

So Sebastian, the grumpy crab, accompanies her. He is her responsible superego. So he also doubles as a substitute for her father, King Triton, Poseidon's son.

Spineless, savage, harpooning fish-eaters, incapable of any feeling! Triton roars about humans. He must learn to let her go on this dangerous desire mission. That despite gallivanting around like a lovesick idiot, she is actually responsible enough to go. That it's her duty to go and find love.

Because he, of course, wants his daughter (his seed) to marry and reproduce. It's just that her departure from the sea represents her departure from his family to Eric's.

Sebastian soothes us parents with the personified idea that we'll always be with our children, even when we're not there.

These moments when I'm cheek to cheek with my daughter experiencing art are so sublime, they hurt.

Like Edmund Burke dramatically shutting his carriage curtains as he bounced his way through the countryside because it hurt to look at so much beauty.

He later writes, *Whatever is fitted in any sort to excite the ideas of pain, and danger, that is to say, whatever is in any sort terrible, or is conversant about terrible objects, or operates in a manner analogous to terror, is a source of the sublime; that is, it is productive of the strongest emotion which the mind is capable of feeling.*

Love is grief. Grief is love.

Jasmine turns her character inside-out when she weaponizes her sexuality to aid Aladdin by pretending to desire to be desired by Jafar. She faux sloughs off her will and impersonates objectification, as though she now wants to be a possession. Jafar becomes so powerful and therefore sexy that he breaks her feminism. He buys it. Jasmine thus becomes the sex object without becoming the sex object, she plays the prize to be won.

But by pretending to be thus she acknowledges that that's how many see her. Just as everyone sees Aladdin as a thief, when really, the system he lives in is corrupt.

It should not be illegal to survive.

Javert is wrong. Jean Valjean was wronged.

It blows my mind how many parents I know who treat their children like objects, like plants or things with instructions.

Americans don't value instructions, they value Master Builders, originality, disruption but.

To fight the sads we lay out art supplies all over the floor, my daughter and me. We watch our movies and make an unholy mess. My daughter makes bright abstract paintings and long story books with pictures, plots, and delightful spellings. We play with colors and shapes, and I weep like mad when Bing Bong disappears, or when Mulan's dad throws Shan Yu's sword to the ground.

When you have good parents, it's hard to fully comprehend the unbearable weight of having bad ones.

Mothers, goddesses of the hearth, sometimes become their homes.

The hollowed feeling in the postpartum period must echo the empty nest that's to come.

In case it needs to be said: Robin Williams is obviously not my uncle.

No more than he is yours.

But what is an uncle?

Yes, yes, bloodline, lineages, marital relations, all that, but.

I have had seven useless uncles, my father's brothers, my mother's half-brothers, and three by marriage. Only three remain. Three disappeared in death, one in divorce. None of them ever felt like family. I had a crush on one for a while, one of those first crushes, the ones that aren't real. He's only a few years older than my husband. His wife is my age. They have a couple of kids. I've never met them.

I deleted my grandmother on Facebook.

My daughter is my mother's age when her father left.

My mother's family exists only on the internet now, through screens. I see their social media photos, their American flag emojis above pixilated memes. Their fangirl crushes on Trump. The prayer chains. Razors in candy, AIDS needles on gas pumps.

The distance between me and them is the distance between representation and reality.

In *Nausicaä of the Valley of the Wind,* when the ohmu charge—the large bugs with their blue eyes gone red—the air is charged, the humans can feel their rage on the wind.

Their justified rage.

Thinking of the fish women storming Marie Antoinette's bed chambers, how they sliced at her bed with their long knives.

A witch by any other name.

When I'm angry, I look like Robin does when he pretends to be a mean pirate in *Hook*. Like I learned how to play angry from a fairy. I look like a cartoon.

My daughter is not afraid of me, not even a little.

I'm Mike Wazowski, I'm not scary.

Yet my parents have always tried to avoid my anger at all costs.

My flaccid anger, like stairs to nowhere.

Cathy Kaboom, they'd laugh. An *Animaniacs* reference. Silly, annoying, comedy, my anger was.

It would bother me, this reduction, this inversion.

I want all of you out there to shut up.
I'm going to live the ways we want to live.
What do you want from me now?
Liver, blood, guts?
The only thing left is madness. (Acker)

Freud says that the psyche longs to repeat the traumatic incident so as to slay the monster, to understand what happened.

In these dark moments we glimpse our own death, and for some, it drives us mad.

This is why children's narratives insist on action, on monsters and villains.

It's why they make evil simple, like a dragon or an orc.

It's why they tell the same story over and over again.

It's why the hero has a thousand faces.

It's why children will want to watch the same movies over and over again.

They're figuring something out. They're overcoming something.

They're fighting something.

We're all fighting something.

The Robin memes love to remind us of that.

Those memes whisper: *He killed himself, you know. Him! Can you believe it? Depression. Him!*

That message has been thoroughly cannibalized.

For a story to hold the child's attention, it must entertain him and arouse his curiosity. But to enrich his life, it must stimulate his imagination; help him to develop his intellect and to clarify his emotions; be attuned to his anxieties and aspirations; give full recognition to his difficulties, while at the same time suggesting solutions to the problems which perturb him. In short, it must at one and the same time relate to all aspects of his personality—and this without ever belittling but, on the contrary, giving full credence to the seriousness of the child's predicaments, while simultaneously promoting confidence in himself and in his future. In all these and many other respects, of the entire "children's literature"—with rare exceptions nothing can be as enriching and satisfying to child and adult alike as the folk fairy tale, writes Bruno Bettelheim.

Who himself was a monster.

Once I heard, his brilliant book became hard to finish.

Because an eidetic trace was left behind, stamped.

Here, I'd like you all to remember Robin's impression of a hotdog.

For joy's sake.

Associations, stimuli, a flow of ideas.

Pop culture piffle, is this book low brow? Derivative, obnoxious and trite? Or pretentious and tries too hard? Academic drivel. Undigested. Plagiarized.

Depends on who you ask. Everything always depends on who you ask.

> What happened that night?

> Something. Nothing. Everything.

No one knows why Robin cut his third wife out of his will. Aside from their shared home, he left all of his tens of millions to his children.

Divorce lawyers use it all the time as a warning, a cautionary tale: *She had no idea.*

There was naturally an icky court battle that ended in a secret settlement.

All three of his wives were not a part of the Hollywood scene.

Almost as though he didn't want to be a part of it either.

Seize the day, boys. Make your lives extraordinary.

Guilt inducing, that one.

Am I living the right way?

How come my grandmother didn't protect her children with her whole body, with her whole being?

How come Alice Munro didn't?

My mother stopped her family's tradition of falling in love with brutal men, with monsters.

Still, I feel cut off from the past. They say this is a white phenomenon, an American phenomenon. This rootlessness, this homelessness. This uncanny existence where celebrities feel more like family than family.

Maybe I'm just stubborn, depressed.

Maybe I'm broken.

Maybe I'm furious.

Maybe I'm lost.

I hale from white trash, they're my bloodline.

The dusty whites, Dave Chappelle calls them. The poor whites. I find them mean and harsh, my people. Their jokes cruel and dangerous. In the middle of a party one adult stood up and abruptly told everyone to *get the fuck off the deck!* Everyone listened, everyone ran. He had strapped a small stick of dynamite to his chair and lit it. Kids were playing on the grass. Somewhere in the distance a couch burned. A couch my mother had given them. This still bothers her. She took it personally. Stuff for my mother is very important and it was as though this couch were an effigy. But they're not that symbolic. They're after their own joy. The carnivalesque.

It belongs to the borderline between art and life. In reality, it is life itself but shaped according to a certain pattern of play...Thus carnival is the people's second life, organized on the basis of laughter, Mikhail Bakhtin writes of the *Carnivalesque.*

A lapse in power structure, carnival is life upside-down, the levity that contains the heavy.

It's a joy hard earned, one with a mean spirit as it's a temporary release and retaliation to a lifetime of oppression.

Like a laughter is the best medicine kind of party.

Patch Adams was right.

Or as Freud posits, the energy released when laughing would normally be used to repress hostile or sexual feelings.

It is said that the real Patch Adams hated the movie made in his honor because, as he said, *the film promised to build our hospital. None of the profits from the film ever came to us, and so, basically forty years into this work, we are still trying to build our hospital.*

Gene Siskel said *I'd rather turn my head and cough than see any part of* Patch Adams *again,* calling Robin's Patch *overbearing, obnoxious, and sanctimonious.*

Robin himself, however, donated much, especially to St. Jude Children's Research Hospital. After his death Adams had said, *I'm enormously grateful for his wonderful performance of my early life, which has allowed the Gesundheit! Institute to continue and expand our work.*

My mother's family has had a lot of close calls, but until recently no one had passed. Everyone had made it. Some really pushed it. They all praise the Lord.

I used to admire my godmother's leather pencil skirts and lacquered nails, the red lips tattooed on her shapely ass. She smoked cigarettes and changed her hair often. There's a video of her dressed as a cat, pretending to blow her own tail for the camera. I thought she was the coolest.

But after many flabby political conversations I saw that there was no rebellion in her. She wasn't intentionally subversive, just after her own joy. A slut for men, for attention. Just another pretty girl happily playing a prize to be won. A *pick me,* they're now called.

I mistook this sluttiness as a political stance. I was wrong. Not even a smidge of Madonna feminism in her, no analytical core.

Assuredly, my aunt would bristle at the word *slut*. She wouldn't understand how that word is very pregnant for me, because in her world it isn't.

Mock quoting her husband—who was to stand for all men here—she took on a redneck voice and said, *I just want a beer and to see something naked.* She was content at being that *something*.

Where is the line between sympathy and pity? Between connection and disgust? Can it be defined?

Madonna often recalls that she was a working-class white girl who saw herself as ugly, as outside the mainstream beauty standard. And indeed what some of us like about her is the way she deconstructs the myth of "natural" white girl beauty by exposing the extent to which it can be and is usually artificially constructed and maintained. She mocks the conventional racist-defined beauty ideal even as she rigorously strives to embody it, writes bell hooks.

The irreality of empathy. The impossibility of it.

I had a doctor once tell me that I was addicted to pain relief.

Aren't you? I asked.

Freud, like Rank, thought that life was an awakening out of a death for which there was no preparation. Life itself was traumatic, because, precisely, it comes from un-being, it comes from death.

That is assuming un-being is the same as death.

The trauma of being born versus the trauma of giving birth.

It's an entry and an exit, my brilliant friend says of birth.

It took me five days to birth my daughter. I was forty-two weeks pregnant. Our time together was up. Neither of us were ready to split apart. Still.

Then they took her away from me for twelve days.

Which means they took me away from her.

This is a trauma, I think, we're both still getting over.

They kept her in the hospital but sent me away.

In my bed, alone, childless, empty, a machine at my breast.

Something went very wrong.

When she finally came home I was sick, so sick.

Our placenta had broken apart, disintegrated, a piece never left me. It, I, became infected. Contaminated. Desperately sad, hating the sounds of the steady electric hum of the breast pump sucking her milk out of me, so I could drive it to her forty minutes away. So they could give her formula anyway.

Vomiting, dizzy, shaking, freezing, burning, sleeping, sweating, crying.

Where is my baby?

Childbed fever was what they used to call it.

Mary Wollstonecraft died from it after birthing Mary Shelley.

I lived, I was given antibiotics.

I took a lot of antibiotics as a kid too.

Remember, only one of Mary Shelley's four children survived.

I am sick of myself, how afraid I am of dying.

How sad I am.

I feel it again, you only get one life.

On his way to pizza my uncle died. His stepson found him in his truck. Something as mundane and wonderful as pizza, then, suddenly, oblivion.

In that sappy, scary afterlife movie, Robin has to travel through suicide hell to pull his wife, who killed herself, into his heaven.

Did that stupid movie occur to him?

It feels impolite to google someone's autopsy, like asking family members, *How?*

It feels like respect, not looking into the details.

LBD is a bitch though, a neurodegenerative disorder characterized by dementia, fluctuations in mental status, hallucinations, and Parkinsonism. The Lewy bodies clump in the brain, which are basically abnormal protein particles. These clusters cause the brain to decay. It's the second most common cause of dementia, following Alzheimer's. Once diagnosed, the lifespan varies from patient to patient, but five to eight years is about average.

Which means, he'd most likely be dead now anyway.

That he knew what it was like to feel his brain dying.

A migraine is more like an electrical storm, but it feels like death, like your eyeball may and should separate from your nerves, that something could be rotting away. Or at least that something is very wrong.

You are not your mother, one of my neurologists would say to me. He was referring to my headaches, their triggers, manifestations, and treatments.

Though the analyst who was bored with me also said this.

Oliver Sacks stresses that the many manifestations of migraine can vary dramatically from one patient to another.

That's who Robin Williams played in *Awakenings*, Oliver Sacks. Significant? Naturally.

Virginia Woolf writes, *to hinder the description of illness in literature, there is the poverty of the language. English, which can express the thoughts of Hamlet and the tragedy of Lear, has no words for the shiver and the headache. It has all grown one way. The merest schoolgirl, when she falls in love, has Shakespeare or Keats to speak her mind for her; but let a sufferer try to describe a pain in his head to a doctor and language at once runs dry. There is nothing ready made for him. He is forced to coin words himself, and, taking his pain in one hand, and a lump of pure sound in the other (as perhaps the people of Babel did in the beginning), so to crush them together that a brand new word in the end drops out. Probably it will be something laughable.*

Reminds me of Irigaray's attempt to do away with language as it only cultivates a male subject.

My mother's and my migraines really are as different as our temperaments, our aesthetics. She has the delicate bone structure of a bird. She is small and beautiful, happiest in summer, playing in the dirt. I like the privacy of winter, hibernating with my papers.

When I was ten, I had an emotional breakdown because my knees were bigger than hers. I take after my father's side. His mother was round as a globe, never wore pants. She was an artist, bipolar, too, I've heard. Would drive in the middle of the night across state lines, leaving her teenage sons to fend for themselves.

Then when I was seventeen, I had another emotional breakdown during Christmas Eve mass. Set to have surgery the next day on a pilonidal cyst that had wrapped its noxious body around my spine, I was stupid scared of the anesthesia, of being at someone else's mercy. Some guy. In the middle of mass, I began throwing up. In the basement, of course, like a lady. I threw up and I cried and my mom tried to calm me down but she didn't know that the night before I had taken half a pill of ecstasy, a *Teletubby*. She didn't know that I was done with my boyfriend (the deacon's son, we were not at a Catholic mass) and was in love with someone else. This felt cataclysmic. Like it mattered. I confessed. I barfed all sorts of words onto the church basement floor with my boyfriend knocking on the door.

A decade later I wrote a collection of short stories about my migraines, where I attempted to translate the pain into emotional narrative arcs. They all had happy endings. The grad students laughed at my happy endings. *But headaches always end,* I said.

How the learned pretend to be allergic to happy endings.

Whatever pain achieves, writes Elaine Scarry, *it achieves in part through its unsharability, and it ensures this unsharability through its resistance to language...Physical pain does not simply resist language but actively destroys it.*

Form as content.

Happy as sad.

Something wonderful, something awful.

For writing to be taken seriously, it must drown in its own pretentious sorrow. Blood on the page and all that.

I cannot believe I, as an egg, was once inside of my mother when she was inside of her mother.

The fantastic chain of mothers, babes to breasts, nurturing, nourishing, protecting.

Ha ha ha, Grace Poole laughs.

Motherless, my mother birthed a new line.

What old histories of men can be rewritten and undone in the story of a new mother? writes my brilliant friend. (Lily Robert-Foley. *The Duty to Presence.*)

Your father is my knight in shining armor, my mother says.

What she means is that he had rescued her from the claws of her family tradition.

In choosing him, she chose herself.

He needed her too, lonely as he was after his father's early cancer death.

Olive Oyl was a clumsy child before she met Popeye, all limbs and noise. Everything was ugly, ugly, ugly including the mirrored reflection in the hat she tries on before her big engagement party to Bluto the brown shirt who snarls and growls like a beast when he eats his meat. Her ugly hat is her ugly idea to marry the town brute.

People have told my mother that she looks like Shelley Long, which as a kid I misinterpreted as Shelley Duvall, and still, that one makes more sense to me.

I cannot imagine how wonderful it is to be blonde. To be covered in fur feels monstrous.

In *Dick Tracy*, all the bad guys' forms reflect their souls, their actions.

In a beautiful fit of clarity Olive runs away to the water, to her subconscious, and into Popeye again. Here, they find the baby. The tag says his name is Sweet Pea.

Holding the baby, Olive Oyl wakes up. She changes, she's a mother now. She cannot marry a brute.

When Popeye and Olive return to the party with Sweet Pea, they must confront her suddenly ex-lover. Bluto works for Popeye's father, functions as Popeye's symbolic father's foot soldier. Bluto, in Bluto's mind, owns Olive and commands Popeye. He and Popeye begin to brawl. No, says the Father, you cannot grow up and become the Father, I will not let you. But the Father also knows he is to dominate the Mother. So Bluto literally breaks Olive Oyl's parents' house with his fists. She once thought him virile and large, but he's actually just a bully, an abuser. Popeye is so lithe and butch, so strong, but only when he has to be. He is the better suitor, he always wins.

Bluto may as well be Bluebeard who murders all his curious wives. Bluebeard, the name, the hair itself, stirs libidinal associations. According to Bruno Bettelheim—who's channeling Freud—Bluebeard confronts the mystery of sexuality, and by dramatizing so bloodily the terror of defloration, helps to assuage it. His victims walk straight into his bed, they want this.

Told once upon a time by the wet nurses and grannies, the myth of Bluebeard also prepares young girls for the horrors of the childbed. *There is a good chance, here, child, is where you will die.*

Though some say *Bluebeard* is more about desire taken to its ultimate conclusion. De Sade's erotism and all.

The war drums of sex.

Not all of you will survive.

Such is the primal drumbeat in *Jumanji*. The call of the wild. Alan Parish, little kid Robin, is beaten up by the Bluto archetype for his emerging sexuality. *Stay away from my girlfriend*, says the bully. Sex games are not for you, you are not old enough, not cool enough. Right after he loses the fight, he hears the jungle's siren song and finds the forbidden game. Right after his father bests him in an argument about his future, the girlfriend will come over and hear the jungle beat too. Then they will play.

In this movie, anger, danger, passion, and sex are all tied together.

When Alan and Sarah first sit down to play *Jumanji*, Alan wants to run away, escape his family and responsibilities, but the drums stop him. The kids play, it's exciting, then quickly terrifying. The game is too much, it consumes Alan, gobbles him up. Sarah only needs to roll a five or an eight to free him, instead, horrified, she flees.

Only she can unlock this pent-up desire.

Twenty-six years later two other kids will hear the jungle song and play. The boy rolls a five and a quite feral, much older Alan emerges from inside the game, or wherever he was. The three of them have to find adult Sarah to finish what they started.

Just like Sweet Pea and the kid in *Dick Tracy,* these two kids function as Alan and Sarah's children. Suddenly the game's bigger than them. They're still afraid to grow up, but they have to do it now, for the kids.

This is the same reason Sad Peter Pan grows up.

(Same reason I did.)

Alan and Sarah's proverbial children are a pair of orphans who have moved into Alan's old house. One lies pathologically, the other refuses to speak. So neither has a voice. Their parents' deaths only just happened. They hear the game and they play. These children didn't hear the jungle beats because their sexualities were awakened, they hear the game because of grief. All children who lose their parents know the cruelty of nature.

Meaning, there are two ways to lose one's innocence: sex or trauma.

If the latter, I'm sorry.

Bluebeard's last wife is like Eve or Pandora. And like the stories of Eve and Pandora, the narrative focuses on the girl's act of disobedience. These are stories about the problems of female curiosity. The sin of being a woman and having a desire for knowledge, or any desire at all. Pandora opens the box and unleashes chaos. Eve is responsible for the Fall of all mankind. So, obviously, girls should act with purity, chastity, and modesty, never ever avarice or lust. Women who desire are dangerous to the social order and must be killed.

Thus, the desire to know makes a woman a madwoman, a witch, a threat.

To want to write is madness.

In order for the heroine to grow up into a normal sexual relationship, she must encounter her Bluebeard then she must kill him, or let her brothers (or Popeye) do it. These good men act as her animus. If she submits to the beast, to desire's ultimate conclusion, she dies.

Or she turns rabid, wild.

Unless she cures him of his beastliness, like Belle.

Thinking now of *8 ½*'s Saraghina and her beastly carnality, her rumba.

In Catholic school, I learned that I both am and am not my body. I am my eternal soul, which is basically my emotional self, who was bullied for having unruly body hair.

Ha ha ha, Grace Poole laughs.

I once purchased a very expensive hour with a laser. I lay like Sleeping Beauty on a vinyl bed, the five-hundred-dollar patch of skin exposed, waiting to be smothered in really cold goo, to be seared. Then a giant, anticipated phallus shot its rays into my body, aiming for the dark black beetles it saw in the goo. Those alien moments of scientifically bettering yourself. Probably giving myself intense cancer doses of radiation.

Do you expect me to talk? No, unwanted body hair, I expect you to die.

I feel like that was a Robin Williams type joke.

One time while I was getting waxed my esthetician told me she was seeing my lover.

We laughed, she and I, what were the odds?

When they searched inside for my daughter, they used the same really cold goo as the laser required. Her tiny body kicking and flailing and spazzing out. How could something so small be so disruptive?

All the seeds for my grandchildren, inside of me inside of her.

Like nesting dolls, we are.

Mary Wollstonecraft: *Taught from infancy that beauty is woman's sceptre, the mind shapes itself to the body, and roaming round its gilt cage, only seeks to adorn its prison.*

Nonetheless, I wanted to be pretty under the laser.

Pretty like Olive Oyl. Like Belle. Like Mom.

There maybe was marijuana in my uncle's system, so I had heard. This wasn't news, but it was said in conspiratorial tones, so the insurance companies wouldn't hear, like the insurance companies were in the fronch room.

What if the insurance companies read this book?

Now he's gone. *Poof.*

I feel the same way about death now as I did at seventeen.

As I spent my early twenties drunk, in love with love, my mother spent them working in the ER. Trauma made her dive into trauma, like a guardian to ward off trauma.

My mother, who used to always say, *Only Cathy can make Cathy happy.*

Why aren't we writing?! My art monster asks me again.

The art monster is as old as I was when Rufus was born.

After I stopped believing in my parents' heaven, the abyss was too abysmal until art. That's where I find solace, unraveling something pretty that somebody took the time to ravel.

Even in Catholic school, I couldn't see religion as anything other than a story. I think I was always an atheist. My father had two nuns for aunts and an archbishop for an uncle. Unofficially, he became the Archbishop of the Moon, as the Diocese of Orlando—which borders Cape Canaveral (where the Apollo 11 mission launched in 1969)—encompassed the territory from which the mission departed.

There is infinite space between art monster and mother.

Stretches to the moon and back, they say.

My mother's family's trauma is not mine. My story is that of a child watching the aftermath, piecing together bits of memories they all wish away. But as an egg, inside my mother, I am a witness. As a body that came from theirs, I have to work on its responses, its constant relapses into scared.

And these panic moments, these migraine nights, aren't theirs, they're mine. This seems what it means to pass down a mental illness or an autoimmune disorder.

It's theirs but it's mine but it's theirs but.

Creation is the opposite of destruction, but one can't be without the other.

Like men and women.

Thinking of Isabelle Huppert masturbating, chanting: *Creation, Destruction. Creation, Destruction.*

Thinking of Isabelle Huppert smashing her hand into broken glass, again to get off.

Thinking of Meryl Streep, draped in a long black veil, pining at the seashore. Catherine's ghost scratching at the windows. Whitney Houston belting Dolly's notes.

That meme again, where the guy gestures to the butterfly: *Is this female desire?*

Life is an endless series of stories.

Art is the opposite of trauma. Safe because it's a reflection. Though sometimes what it reflects is unbearable.

Rufus stumbles now. He walks on his back tiptoes and sleeps under the dishwasher near the heating vent. When he jumps off of the bed he falls. He has trouble getting up. He poops all the time, every hour, everywhere. These hard, tiny poop rocks. He's peeing everywhere too. I can't lock him up, I can't kill him. By what right? I will not put him in a bathroom all night. I tried it once, I sat in front of the gate and cried for an hour.

He's so dehydrated, but he's drinking. I'm not getting it.

A hit, a very palpable hit.

I love him so much, how am I going to say goodbye?

How am I going to leave the vet without him, knees buckling, his bloody paw print in a bag and a whisker I just cut off because I couldn't leave with nothing.

I could not leave with nothing.

Later, they gave me his ashes in a marbled plastic urn with a sticker on the back recommending the company's cremation services, should I need them again. *Until we meet again across the rainbow bridge*, the velvet urn bag says.

We're all going to Valhalla now.

Warrior Rufus. *Snort.* He brought us a dead mouse our other cat killed once.

I put my tarot cards in that bag.

And replaced the sticker with my own, an amethyst cat eating a sandwich. She represents me and Rufus fused, to speak *Steven Universe*.

I'm trying to catch something here.

It really is impossible to own art.

Like trauma, it ripples.

I dreamt about my widowed aunt last night, her farmhouse. A reoccurring dream setting, this busted, infested farmhouse. I really liked it though. It was the stuff of fairy tales. The house changes from dream to dream, but its itness is always the same, there are always many stories. It's often full of animals, as she had a small menagerie. (Which I hear is a trauma response.) As I explore the house, I know I am also searching for a lover, or a secret.

When something ick that should be hidden inside the home is suddenly revealed.

Several lifetimes ago we used to vacation at the lake, my mother's family. We all drove together, a small flock of cars heading north to party. My grandparents had their dog in the cab of their truck. At a pit stop I rushed the window of that imprisoned the dog and forced my love on her. I was ten, or something. She bit me. I remember telling people her jaws were half in and half out of my mouth. I don't remember bleeding. I had been scared, but not angry, and now, not even scarred. When they yelled at the dog, I begged them to stop. Later I learned that my grandfather beat the dog. Late at night, now into my late thirties, this story makes me twitch before I fall asleep.

Robin Williams used to do an impersonation of his id after a joke failed: the man turns into a creature, then an angry child: *Well, fuck you! What do you want from me anyway?!* Then he covers his eyes to cry.

We are all children, trapped inside our insecurities.

I intimately knew Robin as an alien, as Peter Pan, as a frog, and a fruit bat, as a man hiding inside his mother to see his children, as a wild jungle man, a butch sailor, and an all-powerful genie. In these roles he was kind, caring, didactic.

He was avuncular, everything I wished an uncle could be. He was a touch mad, but more importantly, he was there. He talked to me.

He didn't, of course. But we're on the art's realer than real plane now.

You almost never hear Robin talk as himself. He talks as though he's someone else remarking on some aspect of himself. This keeps the light on him without ever shining directly on him. Robin Williams, as we know him, is a series of impersonations, veils. He's an illusion.

On television, he is a closed text. A frame in a frame.

But this hilarious illusion of a person, this semblance of an uncle, was a hit for me, a very palpable hit.

His daughter, Zelda, has a movie out right now about revivifying the dead and the 80s. *Lisa Frankenstein*. Clever.

His eldest son, along with his wife, makes amino acid dietary supplements for mental health. They call them *Mood Chews*. Also clever.

His youngest son stays completely out of the limelight. The cleverest, mayhaps.

More than anything else, my daughter loves how much I make her laugh.

I know how much my mother worries that her trauma is inside of my daughter. As an egg inside me inside her, she was also a witness. They look like each other when they laugh.

I'm trying to be Mirabel, to stay calm and gentle parent my way through emotional dysregulation. I'm very tired.

I don't really know this grandfather story—this father story—but it lives in my bones.

It's theirs but it's mine but it's theirs but.

It lives in my nerves when I get into arguments with all the men I've known. Each time they yell and drown in their own black miseries, I see the sadness in the rage and I am left holding pieces of my ancestry like shards of a broken plate.

I think of Connie Corleone curled up on the bathroom floor while her husband beats her, calls her a brat as though.

My heart burns, and my nerves buzz, and I think about how I used to throw up in my sleep.

I think about my cowardly grandfather. So tough and mean, hurting little girls.

I miss Rufus so God damn much.

At home, I look out of my windows and I don't want to be anywhere else.

Here with my kin, watching a movie, the snow is blue and calm.

That's the good stuff.

It'll quite possibly be a Robin Williams movie.

His last performing words were: *Smile, my boy, it's sunrise.*

How lovely, how apt.

The darkness is over.

Happiness can be found, even in the darkest of times, if one only remembers to turn on the light, Dumbledore, meaning J.K. Rowling says.

Estragon: *We always find something, eh Didi, to give us the impression we exist?*

Mork: *I don't know how much value I have in this universe but I do know I've made a few people happier than they would've been without me. As long as I know that, I'm as rich as I ever need to be.*

I'm lucky to know peace.

I'm lucky I get to make a safe home for my kin.

Lucky to be with them, watching cartoons, and laughing like crazy.

...

References

Acker, Kathy. *Blood and Guts in High School*. Grove Press, 1984.

Adams, Patch. Transform Symposium. Mayo Clinic. 2010.

Allen, Woody, dir. *Annie Hall*. A Jack Rollins and Charles H. Joffe Production, 1977.
-----. *Deconstructing Harry*. Sweetland Films, 1997.

Allers, Roger, and Rob Minkoff, dirs. *The Lion King*. Walt Disney Feature Animation, 1994.

Altman, Robert, dir. *Popeye*. Paramount Pictures, 1980.

Atwood, Margaret. *The Year of the Flood*. Bloomsbury Publishing, 2009.

Austen, Jane. *Persuasion*. John Murray, 1818.

—————. *Pride and Prejudice*. T. Egerton, Whitehall, 1813.

Beckett, Samuel. *Waiting for Godot.* 1953.
—————. *The Unnamable*. Grove Press, 1958.

Bellamy, Dodie. "Phone Home" and "The Bandaged Lady." *When the Sick Rule the World*. Semiotext(e)/Active Agents, 2015.

Bettelheim, Bruno. *The Uses of Enchantment: The Meaning and Importance of Fairy Tales*. Thames & Hudson, 1977.

Beyoncé. *Lemonade*. Parkwood Entertainment and Columbia Records, 2016.

Boyer, Anne. Keynote address at AUTO-, 2019.

Branagh, Kenneth, dir. *Hamlet.* Castle Rock Entertainment, 1996.

Briggs, Kate. *This Little Art*. Fitzcarraldo Editions, 2017.

Brönte, Charlotte. *Jane Eyre*. Smith, Elder & Co., 1847.

Brönte, Emily. *Wuthering Heights*. Thomas Cautley Newby, 1847.

Burke, Edmund. *A Philosophical Enquiry into the Origin of Our Ideas of the Sublime and Beautiful*. Prairie State Books, 1968.

Bush, Jared, and Byron Howard, dirs. *Encanto*. Walt Disney Studios Motion Pictures, 2021.

Carson, Anne. *Eros the Bittersweet*. Dalkey Archive Essentials, 2022.
-----. *Glass and God*. Vintage/Ebury, 1998.

Caruth, Cathy. *Unclaimed Experience: Trauma, Narrative, and History*. Johns Hopkins University Press, 2016.

Casper, Barbara, dir. *Who's Afraid of Kathy Acker?* 2008.

Cassavetes, John, dir. *A Woman Under the Influence*. Faces International Films, 1974.

Cixous, Hélène. *Stigmata: Escaping Texts*. Trans. Eric Prenowitz, Keith Cohen, and Catherine A.F. MacGillivray. Routledge Classics, 2005.
-----. "The Laugh of the Medusa." Trans. Keith Cohen and Paula Cohen. 1976.
-----. "Sorties." *The Newly Born Woman*. Trans. Betsy Wing. Theory and History of Literature, Volume 24, 1986.

Columbus, Chris, dir. *Mrs. Doubtfire*. 20th Century Fox, 1993.

Cook, Barry and Tony Bancroft, dirs. *Mulan*. Walt Disney Feature Animation, 1998.

Coppola, Francis Ford, dir. *Jack*. Hollywood Pictures, 1996.
-----. *The Godfather*. Paramount Pictures, 1972.

Costandi, Mo. *Pregnant 9/11 Survivors Transmitted Trauma to Their Children.* The Guardian, 2011.

The Daily Beast. *Kevin Smith on Coining 'Bennifer' and Trying to Save His Hero Stan Lee.* 2021.

Dante, Alighieri. *The Divine Comedy.* Trans. John Ciardi. Berkley, 2003.

DeVito, Danny, dir. *Death to Smoochy.* Warner Bros. Pictures, 2002.

Docter, Pete, dir. *Inside Out.* Pixar Animation Studios. 2015.

DuVall, Shelley. *Faerie Tale Theatre.* Gaylord Production Company, 1982-1987.

Faust, Lauren. *My Little Pony: Friendship Is Magic.* Hasbro, 2010-2019.

Freud, Sigmund. *Leonardo da Vinci and A Memory of His Childhood.* 1910. W. W. Norton & Company, 1990.

-----. *The Uncanny*. 1919. Trans. David McLintock. Penguin Classics, 2003.

Gilbert, Sandra M., and Susan Gubar. *The Madwoman in the Attic: The Woman Writer and the Nineteenth-Century Literary Imagination*. Yale University Press, 1979, 2000.

Gilliam, Terry, dir. *The Adventures of Baron Munchausen*. Columbia Pictures, 1989.
-----. *The Fisher King*. TriStar Pictures, 1991.

Greno, Nathan, and Byron Howard, dirs. *Tangled*. Walt Disney Animation Studios, 2010.

Groening, Matt. *The Simpsons*. Gracie Films and 20th Television, 1989-.

Fellini, Federico, dir. *8½*. Cineriz, 1963.

Fowles, Jon; and Karel Reisz, dirs. *The French Lieutenant's Woman*. United Artists, 1981.

Heidegger, Martin. *Being and Time: A Translation of Sein und Zeit.* Trans. Joan Stambaugh. State University of New York Press, 1996.

Henson, Jim, dir. *Fraggle Rock.* Henson Associates, 1983-1987.

-----. *Labyrinth.* TriStar Pictures, 1986.

-----, in collaboration with et al. *Sesame Street.* Sesame Workshop, 1969-.

-----. *The Frog Prince.* Muppets, Inc., 1971.

Herrick, Robert. "To the Virgins, To Make Much of Time." 1648.

hooks, bell. *All About Love: New Visions.* Harper, 1999.

-----. "Power to the Pussy: We Don't Wanna Be Dicks in Drag." Outlaw Culture. Routledge Classics, 1994.

Horkheimer, Max, and Theodor W. Adorno. *Dialectic of Enlightenment (Cultural Memory in the Present).* Trans. Edmund Jephcott. Stanford University Press, 2007.

Houston, Whitney. *I Will Always Love You*. *The Bodyguard - Original Soundtrack Album*, 1992. Written by Dolly Parton, 1974.

Hugo, Victor. *Les Misérables*. A. Lacroix, Verboeckhoven & Cie., 1862.

Jackson, Shirley. "The Lottery." The New Yorker, 1948.

Jackson, Wilfred, Hamilton Luske, and Clyde Geronimi, dirs. *Cinderella*. Walt Disney Productions, 1950.

-----. *Peter Pan*. Walt Disney Productions, 1953.

Jelinek, Elfriede; and Michael Haneke, dir. *The Piano Teacher*. MK2, 2001.

Johnston, Joe, dir. *Jumanji*. TriStar Pictures, 1995.

Jung, Carl. *The Archetypes and the Collective Unconscious*. 1959. Trans. R.F.C. Hull. Routledge. 1991.

Kasdan, Jake, dir. *Jumanji: Welcome to the Jungle.* Columbia Pictures, 2017.

Kaysen, Susanna; and James Mangold, dir. *Girl, Interrupted.* Columbia Pictures, 1999.

Klein, Melanie. *Love, Guilt and Reparation: And Other Works 1921-1945.* Free Press, 2002.
-----. *The Importance of Symbol-Formation in the Development of the Ego.* Int. J. Psycho-Anal., 11:24-39, 1930.

Kristeva, Julia. *Powers of Horror: An Essay on Abjection.* Columbia University Press, 1982.

Kroyer, Bill, dir. *FernGully: The Last Rainforest.* Kroyer Films Inc., 1992.

Kundera, Milan. *The Unbearable Lightness of Being.* Harper & Roe, 1984.

Lacan, Jacques. *Anxiety: The Seminar of Jacques Lacan, Book X*. Trans. Cormac Gallagher from unedited French typescripts.

Lee, Jennifer and Chris Buck dirs. *Frozen*. Walt Disney Animation Studios, 2013.

Leoncavallo, Ruggero. *Pagliacci*. 1892.

Levinson, Barry, dir. *Good Morning Vietnam*. Touchstone Pictures. 1987.

Levy, Shawn, dir. *Night at the Museum*. 20th Century Fox, 2006.

Loy, Mina. *Feminist Manifesto*. 1914.
-----. *The Lost Lunar Baedeker: Poems of Mina Loy*. Farrar, Straus and Giroux, 1997.

MacFarlane, Seth. *Family Guy*. Fuzzy Door, 20th Television, 1999-2002; 2005-.

Malory, Sir Thomas. *Le Morte d'Arthur*. William Caxton, 1485.

Marshall, Gary, Joe Glauberg, and Dale McRaven. *Mork & Mindy*. Henderson Production Company, Inc.; Miller-Milkis Productions; Miller-Milkis-Boyett Productions; Paramount Television, 1978-1982.

Marshall, Penny, dir. *Awakenings*. Columbia Pictures, 1990.

Martin, George R.R. *Song of Ice and Fire Series*. Random House Worlds, 2013.

Mayfield, Les, dir. *Flubber*. Walt Disney Pictures, 1997.

Miller, George, dir. *Happy Feet*. Warner Bros. Pictures, 2006.

Miranda, Lin-Manuel. *Hamilton*. 2015.

Miyazaki, Hayao, dir. *Kiki's Delivery Service*. Studio Ghibli, 1989.
-----. *Nausicaä of the Valley of the Wind*. Studio Ghibli, 1984.

—―—. *Spirited Away*. Studio Ghibli, 2001.

Musker, John and Ron Clements, dirs. *Aladdin*. Walt Disney Pictures, 1992.

—―—. *The Little Mermaid*. Walt Disney Feature Animation. 1989.

—―—. *The Princess and the Frog*. Walt Disney Studios Motion Pictures, 2009.

Naim, Omar, dir. *The Final Cut*. Lions Gate Films, 2004.

Nichols, Mike, dir. *The Birdcage*. United Artists, 1996.

Nietzsche, Friedrich. *The Will to Power*. Trans. Walter Kaufmann. Vintage, 1968.

Nin, Anaïs. *The Diary of Anaïs Nin, Vol. 1: 1931-1934*. Mariner Books Classics, 1969.

—―—. *House of Incest*. Swallow Press, 1947.

—―—. *Incest: From "A Journal of Love": The Unexpurgated Diary of Anaïs Nin, 1932-1934*. Mariner Books Classics, 1993.

Norwood, Tyler, dir. *Robin's Wish*. Vertical, 2020.

Offill, Jenny. *Dept. of Speculation*. Vintage Contemporaries, 2014.

Oz, Frank, dir. *Little Shop of Horrors*. Warner Bros., 1986.

Petersen, Wolfgang, dir. *The Neverending Story*. Warner Bros., 1984.

Pullman, Philip. *His Dark Materials*. Scholastic. 1995-2000.

Rank, Otto. *The Trauma of Birth*. Dover Publications, 1924.

Rich, Adrienne. *Women and Honor: Some Notes on Lying*. Motherroot Publications, 1977.

Robert-Foley, Lily. *The Duty to Presence*. Presses Universitaires de Rouen, 2022.

Romanek, Mark, dir. *One Hour Photo*. Fox Searchlight Pictures, 2002.

Rowling, J.K. *Harry Potter*. Bloomsbury, 1997-2007.

Ruegger, Tom. *Animaniacs*. Amblin Entertainment. 1993-1998.

Russell, David O, dir. *I Heart Huckabees*. Qwerty Films, 2004.

Russell, Francey. "What It Means to Watch." Boston Review, 2022.

Sacks, Oliver. *Migraine*. Vintage, 1999.

Sartre, Jean Paul. *The Emotions: Outline of a Theory*. Trans. Bernard Frechtman. Philosophical Library/Open Road, 2012.
-----. *The Imaginary: A phenomenological psychology of the imagination*. Trans. Jonathan Webber. Routledge. 2004.
-----. *Nausea*. Trans. Lloyd Alexander. 1949. Penguin Modern Classics. 2000.

Scanlon, Suzanne. *Committed: On Meaning and Madwomen.* Vintage, 2024.

Scarry, Elaine. *The Body in Pain: The Making and Unmaking of the World.* Oxford University Press, 1987.

Schwartz, Niles. *Retrieving the Grail: Robin Williams and "The Fisher King".* RogerEbert.com, 2014.

Shakespeare, William. *Hamlet.* Sometime between 1599 and 1601.

Shelley, Mary. *Frankenstein.* Lackington, Hughes, Harding, Mavor & Jones, 1818.

Spielberg, Steven, dir. *Hook.* TriStar Pictures, 1991.

Tatar, Maria. *Hard Facts of Grimms' Fairy Tales: Expanded Edition.* Princeton Classics, 2019.

Theweleit, Klaus. *Male Fantasies, Vol. 1: Women, Floods, Bodies, History.* Trans. Chris Turner, Stephen Conway, and Erica Carter. University of Minnesota Press, 1987.

Tolkien, J.R.R. *The Hobbit.* Allen & Unwin, 1937.
-----. *The Lord of the Rings.* Allen & Unwin, 1954-1955.

Trousdale, Gary and Kirk Wise, dirs. *Beauty and the Beast.* Walt Disney Feature Animation, 1991.

Ward, Vincent, dir. *What Dreams May Come.* Interscope Communications, 1998.

Warner, Marina. *From the Beast to the Blonde: On Fairy Tales and Their Tellers.* Farrar, Straus and Giroux, 1996.

Wedge, Chris, dir. *Robots.* 20th Century Fox Animation, 2005.

Weir, Peter, dir. *Dead Poet's Society.* Buena Vista Pictures Distribution, 1989.

White, T.H. *The Once and Future King*. Collins, 1958.

Whitman, Walt. "Song of Myself." *Leaves of Grass*. 1855.

Woolf, Virginia. *A Room of One's Own*. Harcourt Brace Jovanovich Publishers. 1929.
-----. *On Being Ill*. Paris Press, 2012.

Zambreno, Kate. *Heroines*. Semiotext(e)/Active Agents, 2012.

Zenovich, Maria, dir. *Robin Williams: Come Inside My Mind*. HBO, 2018.

About the Author

Cathy Borders is the author of *The Tarot for Writing Project*, a free online tool that teaches writing through the Tarot, and teaches the Tarot through analogy using fairy tales, myths, classic literature, philosophy, film, and cartoons. She is also the author of the experimental romance, *A Suburb of Monogamy*. As a fictional translation of Roland Barthes's *A Lover's Discourse*, *Suburb* is about the invention, withdrawal, and body of a liaison. Her short fiction and academic essays can be found in various lit journals across the internet, she's even won a few honorable mentions here and there. She's a book midwife, story therapist, and also the founder of The Republic of Letters—an online lit hub dedicated to helping local authors get their books into the hands of local readers—where she runs the quarterly reading series, Water Street Writers. She has an MFA in Creative Writing from the New School in New York and a Bachelor's degree in English literature and critical theory from the University of Iowa. She lives in the forest with her husband and two daughters where she writes, edits, and walks.

>CathyBorders.com
>@Story_Therapist

www.ingramcontent.com/pod-product-compliance
Lightning Source LLC
Chambersburg PA
CBHW020930090426
42736CB00010B/1100